More Th

GW00367527

Also available from Marshall Pickering

WINNING IS NOT ENOUGH
Stuart Weir and Andrew Wingfield Digby

More Than Champions

Sports stars' secrets of success

STUART WEIR

Foreword by Kriss Akabusi

Marshall Pickering
An Imprint of HarperCollinsPublishers

Marshall Pickering is an Imprint of
HarperCollins*Religious*
Part of HarperCollins*Publishers*
77–85 Fulham Palace Road, London W6 8JB

First published in Great Britain
in 1993 by Marshall Pickering

1 3 5 7 9 10 8 6 4 2

A catalogue record for this book is
available from the British Library

ISBN 0 551 02771–1

Printed and bound in Great Britain by
The Guernsey Press Co. Ltd, Guernsey, Channel Islands

For the Christians in Sport staff –
a great team to play for

Andrew Wingfield Digby
Graham Daniels
Joy Williams
Julia Sammons
Helen Nunn

CONTENTS

ACKNOWLEDGEMENTS

Grateful thanks are recorded to a number of people who have helped this book see the light of day: to colleagues Andrew and Graham for reading the manuscript and making many constructive criticisms, to Catherine Butcher for advice on particular aspects, to the many people within the Christians in Sport network who were willing to talk to me and whose experiences are recorded in the book.

Thanks too to the many sportspeople whom I have never met, whose opinions are quoted from books and newspapers – I hope that I have misrepresented no one.

Acknowledgement is made of the stimulation of two books, referred to in more than a few places: *Sport and Religion*, edited by Shirl J. Hoffman, published by Human Kinetics (Illinois) 1992, and *Sporting Excellence: A study of sport's high achievers*, by David Hemery, published by Collins Willow 1986. Many of the quotations in this book which are acknowledged to the original sources are from articles reproduced in *Sport and Religion*.

Thanks to Christine Smith of HarperCollins*Religious* for the opportunity to write the book, and to Helen Nunn for willingly re-typing the bits which I accidentally deleted.

I am constantly grateful for the support of Northwood Hills Evangelical Church during seventeen years of membership, particularly Roger Pearce and Jeffery Wilson for consistent encouragement, the Wednesday 7 a.m. prayer meeting and Angela Morgan in anticipation of more ingenious ways of selling the book on her bookstall.

Finally thanks to my family: Lynne, Christine and Jonathan (plus guinea pigs Fluffy and Fudge) for the sacrifices made while I worked on this book. I hope you think it was worth it!

STUART WEIR
Christians in Sport
PO Box 93
Oxford OX2 7YP

FOREWORD

At the first warm weather training camp in my athletics career, in Bolzano in the Northern Italian Alps in 1979, I picked up a quote from Alexander Pope, the English poet from the Age of Reason: "Blessed are they who expect nothing for they will not be disappointed." I wrote this down in my training diary and determined that this would be my approach to winning in athletics. So I began my track and field career. Train, compete and be happy. "Laissez-faire" must rule the day. So it did; within five years I was competing at the highest level a sportsman can achieve – the Olympic Games.

Pierre de Coubertin, the founder of the modern Olympic Games, seemed to amplify Pope's precept when he said, "The important thing in the Olympic Games is not to win, but to take part; the important thing in life is not the triumph but the struggle; the essential thing is not having conquered but to have fought well."

However I was soon to learn the folly of these words in the modern era. I won a silver medal in the British relay quartet and made the semi-final as an individual. I certainly had not expected the silver and had only hoped that I would make the semis. I was ecstatic with jubilation.

On my return home I was to learn from experience a cruel truth. In world class sport, winning is everything. Coming second means nothing. Marketing managers and public relations officers want winners; sponsors and advertisers want winners; armchair critics and enthusiastic punters want winners. "Win, win, win," say the media moguls, "and we will make you stars." Sport, it seemed, was definitely more than a game.

Eight years later, I was to be in my third Olympic Games. As European and Commonwealth Champion in my own right and World Champion with the aid of my relay colleagues, I went to the games with one thing on my mind – "Champion Olympique". I was not in my best physical shape but mentally I was prepared. I feared none of my competitors but respected them all. You have to be good to make an Olympic final, and I was up against the world's greatest.

As I blasted from my blocks I felt fine and things were going great until about halfway round. Then Kevin Young, a hitherto unheralded outsider from the USA, came blowing past me between hurdles three and four; by hurdle five he was a full five metres up, not including the stagger. My dream was becoming a nightmare. A bad one! I kept on working hard. Into the home straight and there was still something to run for – only Kevin and Winthrop Graham were ahead of me, albeit eight metres in Kevin's case. Blam! I crossed the line and the big screen flashed, "Kevin Young – New world record!" Kevin had just become the fastest man in history. Back in third place I once again became the fastest man in British history. At that moment I learnt a lesson that would stay with me the rest of my life: I was never going to be Olympic Champion.

For many reading this foreword, an Olympic medal of any description will be beyond their wildest dreams. But one thing that Kevin and I had in common that day was that we had both given of our very best effort. My time and position represented the very best that I could be on that day. That is something that we can *all* aspire to. To do whatever we choose, to the best of our ability, and in so doing to be content. Both Pope and de Coubertin were right: aspire to many things, expect nothing, fight, struggle and play to win, but not at all costs; for sport, after all, should be no more than a game.

Becoming a Christian changed my attitude to athletics. Before I was a Christian I felt that I was only as good as my last race. If I ran badly I was a nobody. As a Christian I came to realize that I could glorify God no matter where I finished. I realized that God had given me the ability and it was just up to me to do my best. If I was to win that was good but if I was to come last, "C'est la vie".

I still want to win and want to do my best. By

winning I can bring glory to God – but I can also glorify God if I don't win.

In the 1992 Olympics, I was just as hungry as anyone and I wanted to win an Olympic gold medal. I thought I could do it. Coming third was a real disappointment, but I was still able to give thanks to God for his goodness in getting me there. Being a Christian helped me to accept the achievement of coming third and keep it in perspective.

The stories in this book illustrate that we can all be champions. Crossing the finishing line first and being the best we can be are not the same thing.

Best of all, in God's eyes, we can never lose.

KRISS AKABUSI
January 1993

14

Introduction

There is a story about a group of Martians who were sent down to study life on Earth. They reported back to the hysterical laughter of their fellow Martians that they had seen the strangest thing.

Eleven men dressed in white formed a circle in a large field. Two men with padding strapped on to their legs and body came on to the field carrying a piece of willow. One of the original eleven hurled a round leather object which one of the other two men tried to hit with his piece of willow. What made it the more remarkable was that thousands of these earthlings came to watch this strange spectacle. Those who couldn't get there watched it on their televisions!

Fans of Michael Bentine know of course that cricket is really a form of rain dance in which the priests dress all in white and gather round the two altars of three holy stumps which they have carefully positioned in the temple. Then when the two high priests in their special long white coats appear, the rain floods down!

To anyone from outside our culture our obsession with sport would be hard to understand. Nonetheless the importance of sport in our society cannot be denied. The morale of the entire country can rise or fall according to the success or failure of our national teams.

We are fascinated by the stars of sport. By the millions we congregate in arenas and stadia to cheer them to victory. By the tens of millions we watch them on television. Their professional and private lives are chronicled in newspapers, magazines, on radio and television. Business loves them, because through their visibility and influence they can sell us products ranging from razors to racing cars, breakfast cereals to window frames. When they speak we listen. What they wear, we wear, what they do, we do. They are examples and role models to millions.

Sport reaches parts of society that other activities cannot reach. When Sunderland won the FA Cup in 1973 (as a second division side) it was said that productivity in local industry rose in the euphoric aftermath of the success. Equally a poor England performance in an important football international, with the work-force reading their tabloid papers which portray the England manager as a turnip-head, is likely to have the opposite effect on production levels. In Bill Shankly's memorable words: "Football is not a matter of life and death, it is more important than that."

Definition

Sport is more easily understood than defined. The definition used by the Council of Europe is:

Sport means all forms of physical activity, which, through casual or organized participation, aim at expressing or improving physical fitness and mental wellbeing, forming social relationships or obtaining results in competition at all levels.

The British Sports Council has a broader view going beyond the Council of Europe to include four categories:

1. Competitive sport (e.g. football, tennis, golf).
2. Physical recreation (non-competitive activities usually conducted on an informal basis, e.g. walking/hiking, cycling, boating).
3. Aesthetic activities (e.g. movement and dance).
4. Conditioning activities (those activities engaged in primarily for health and fitness benefits, e.g. aerobics, weight training, exercise to music).

A recent Sports Council report, "Women and Sport", quoted the view of Gary Whannel (*Blowing the whistle: the politics of sport*, 1983):

English sport is one of the most distinctly male of all social institutions. Sport has been played more by men, watched by men and crucially controlled by men.

In refuting this view the Council suggested that Whannel's definition of sport as "formally organized competitive sport" was inadequate. The definition needed to include "activities where there is a great emphasis on individual health and wellbeing and informal social contacts". This helpful broadening of the definition of sport is echoed in the Sports Council's own slogan, "Sport for All".

Peter Ballantine's definition in his Grove Booklet *Sport – the opiate of the people* is "a particular way of using leisure time in a combination of physical and mental skills in a competitive way leading to a set of aims/goals by which a contest is won or lost". However this definition is inadequate in two respects. The reference to "leisure time" excludes all professional sport. The insistence that sport must result in a win or a loss excludes three of the Sports Council's four categories.

The fun-run in the local park, with its emphasis on participation, not on winning, is as legitimately "sport" as the Olympic 100 metres final. One event which has succeeded in bringing both together is the London Marathon in which the elite runners battle for first place and 25,000 others run for the satisfaction of the participation. In the London Marathon all receive a prize for their participation.

Arthur Holmes has noted how the idea of play

permeates all levels of society. Sociologists talk about "the roles people play", in economics one "plays the market", in politics there is the "election race", "front runners" with their "game plans", in philosophy Wittgenstein talks of "language games" and in mathematics there is "game theory". Even Shakespeare made his contribution with the line: "All the world's a stage, and all the men and women merely players."

History of sport

The origins of sport can probably be found in re-creating the hunt. Archery, throwing the javelin or spear, running, etc., were all among the professional skills of the ancient hunter. There is also the military influence. Physical fitness, strength and toughness derived from competition were important military attributes. The first organizers of sport on a systematic basis were the ancient Greeks.

Many of the global sports were invented in Britain. The mere mention of St Andrews, Twickenham or Lords, for example, conjure up a magic around the world.

Sport in the Ancient World

The Olympic Games trace their origins back to 776 B.C. in Greece. Other evidence of sport in the ancient world can be found in the Old Testament.

While the life style of the majority of the Hebrews probably left little time for physical sport, there is evidence of running, throwing, hunting, weightlifting, wrestling, javelin throwing and archery being practised. David would have been a hot favourite for the sling-and-five-stones target-shooting gold medal, even if Saul might not have made the javelin-throwing team.

There is also the statement in Zechariah 8:5 that "the streets shall be full of boys and girls playing". Play is part of God's plan for the restored Israel. Play and recreation are gifts from God.

In the New Testament almost all the references to sport are to Greek athletic contests. Paul, in particular, often makes reference to the games in general. In 1 Corinthians Paul calls attention to the vigorous training of the athlete. The Christian is challenged to follow the example of the athlete and to strive for the crown which lasts.

Do you know that in a race all the runners run, but only one gets the prize? Run in such a way as to get the prize. Everyone who competes in the games goes into strict training. They do it to get a crown that will not last; but we do it to get a crown that will last for ever. Therefore I do not run like a man running aimlessly; I do not fight like a man beating the air. No, I beat my body and make it my slave so that after I have preached to others, I myself will not be disqualified for the prize.

1 Corinthians 9:24–27

Here Paul uses metaphors from the games familiar to all his readers and as countless preachers have done since, he contrasts the disciple accepted by athletes competing for an earthly prize with Christian failure to grasp the demands made on those who seek the highest of all callings.

In several places Paul urges the Christian to persevere in order to gain his/her reward in Heaven, comparing this to the athlete training to gain the prize in the Games.

Now there is in store for me the crown of righteousness, which the Lord, the righteous Judge, will award to me on that day – and not only to me, but also to all who have longed for his appearing.

2 Timothy 4:8

The same thought is found in 1 Peter 5:4.

And when the Chief Shepherd appears, you will receive the crown of glory that will never fade away.

Elsewhere weight shed by the athlete in training is compared with sin.

Therefore, since we are surrounded by such a great cloud of witnesses, let us throw off everything that hinders and the sin that so easily entangles, and let us run with perseverance the race marked out for

us. Let us fix our eyes on Jesus, the author and
perfecter of our faith, who for the joy set before
him endured the cross, scorning its shame, and sat
down at the right hand of the throne of God.

Hebrews 12:1, 2

Another sporting reference comes in Philippians 3:13,
14.

Brothers, I do not consider myself yet to have taken
hold of it. But one thing I do: Forgetting what is
behind and straining towards what is ahead, I press
on towards the goal to win the prize for which God
has called me heavenwards in Christ Jesus.

Paul also referred in places to the Christian life in
terms of running a race, e.g. Galatians 2:2, "But I did
this privately to those who seemed to be leaders, for
fear that I was running or had run my race in vain";
Galatians 5:7, "You were running a good race. Who
cut in on you and kept you from obeying the truth?"
and Philippians 2:16, ". . . as you hold out the word
of life – in order that I may boast on the day of Christ
that I did not run or labour for nothing".

From these references there could not be argued
to be a Biblical view of sport. It is rather that Paul
and the other New Testament writers recognize sport
as an integral part of the society of their day and
therefore see it as an obvious source of imagery in
describing the Christian faith.

However, it should be noted that the Bible has a

high view of the human body. There is none of the body-soul dualism found in Greek thought. Man is a unity. The very fact of the incarnation dignifies the human body. That Jesus healed human bodies confirms this. The clear conclusion from this is that the human body is good and wholesome.

Sport in modern society

In the modern age, sport is a hobby, a recreation. It has a psychological, physical and recreational value. It can socialize us and discipline us. It has even been suggested that the family that plays together stays together.

The European Sports Conference Charter described sport as "an inalienable right of every person". It is also a job. It is big business. The latest statistics indicate that some 28 million people, half the entire British population, take part in sport or recreation at least once a month. Millions more watch or follow sport. Sporting successes – whether national or local – give us pleasure and pride.

In a leaflet *The Case for Sport*, published by the four UK Sports Councils, it is stated:

Sport is its own justification. It is a vital element in our national culture. In addition, sport:

— contributes to greater fitness, better health and a sense of personal wellbeing;

— plays a vital part in a rounded education for children;

— offers opportunities for varied experiences and new fellowship in the community; it offers particular fulfilment and health benefits to people with disabilities;

— generates nearly £9 billion of financial expenditure for the economy;

— provides almost 400,000 jobs;

— promotes and enhances Britain's standing in the world.

The cynic might add, "They would say that, wouldn't they?" and wonder whether Britain's standing in the world has been enhanced by the hooliganism which is often associated with the national football team or the drug-taking scandals which are so prevalent today. The cynical, win-at-all-costs philosophy, the commercialism which seems to dominate, might also be seen to mitigate against the positive view of sport.

Inevitably sport gets entangled in the political arena. Sport is used by nations to promote their international credibility – for example in East Germany in the 70s and 80s. Inevitably too, sport has been the target of pressure groups. The pressure of the outside world on South Africa to abandon its apartheid policies focused much more on sporting links than on business. In their quest for a homeland the Palestinian terrorists saw the 1972 Olympics as a legitimate target. Sportspeople often argue that politics should be kept out of sport. In our complex modern world, that seems an unrealistic aspiration.

While the slogan may be "Sport for All" there are many who feel that women, who comprise 52 per cent of the British population, do not get a fair crack of the whip. There is no doubt that women are in general at a disadvantage compared to men when it comes to opportunity to participate in sport.

As sport is excluded from the provisions of the 1975 Sex Discrimination Act, sports clubs are able to continue as single-sex clubs or with unequal terms of membership. Without doubt this has worked to the disadvantage of women.

Professional sport

Dan O'Brien was the World Number 1 in the decathlon (ten track and field events completed in two days) in 1992. He entered the US Olympic trials as firm favourite. He led the competition at the halfway stage. In the pole vault it all went wrong. Three times he failed to clear the bar at a height which was easily within his capabilities. He finished 11th and missed the Olympics. Reebok cancelled a $20-million advertising campaign which was to have featured the duel between O'Brien and another athlete at the Olympics. Don't try telling O'Brien that it's only a game!

For the man in the street, sport is his hobby, his

recreation. He may endure a boring job from Monday to Friday for his Saturday morning round of golf, game of football or whatever.

This is, however, a million miles from the experience of the professional who talks of his sport as "going to work". The last thing the professional golfers are likely to take with them on holiday are their golf clubs.

The pressures to succeed are enormous, greater in some sports than in others. If your goal is the Olympics, then failure means four years' work wasted and another four before there is a chance to have another go. This theme will be developed more fully when we look at the anatomy of a champion and the life style of the sportsperson. However it is important at this stage to recognize the distinction between sport for fun and professional sport.

As George Orwell has put it:

> Serious sport has nothing to do with fair play. It is bound up with hatred, jealousy, boastfulness, disregard of all rules and sadistic pleasure in witnessing violence: in other words it is war minus the shooting.

In this book we shall see that it is possible for a Christian to have a much more positive attitude to sport than Orwell's, more in tune perhaps with Calvin's view of the world as the "theatre of God's glory".

Christians and sport

The Christian Church has had over the years an ambivalent attitude to sport. Originating in the philosophy of J. J. Rousseau, the doctrine of "Muscular Christianity" became influential in the last century. This was a view that there was positive moral influence in physical exercise and sport and that as competitive sport had an ethical basis, training in moral behaviour on the playing field was transferable to the outside world.

> Unselfishness, justice, health: these were the type of ideals that were manifest in sport, but also in any proper Christian society.
>
> Peter McIntosh, *Fair Play*

Manifestations of Muscular Christianity included the development of sport in the public schools and the encouragement of football among the working classes. In fact something like a quarter of today's English professional football teams were founded by churches – for example, Queen's Park Rangers were originally "St Jude's", Southampton started life as "Southampton St Mary" and Fulham as "Fulham St Andrew's".

In later years the Church tended to be suspicious of sport, reflecting perhaps the Puritan view that involvement in sport was a "fearfull ingratitude and provocation unto the glorious God". This negative view of sport was probably based partly on external factors such as the association with drinking and gambling. Moreover much sport takes place on a Sunday. Sport was also seen as leading to fanaticism, exposing one's body unnecessarily to injury, and also as a distraction from the more pressing duties of the Christian.

It may seem strange, however, that Christian leaders who encourage people not to get carried away with the amount of time devoted to sport do not seem to have the same reservations about literature, art, classical music, etc.

In recent years a movement has developed to promote a Christian presence in sport. Role models have emerged to show that it is possible to be a Christian and to reach the top in sport.

The message is well encapsulated in that scene from the film *Chariots of Fire*, when Eric Liddell's thoughts as he runs are "God made me for a purpose, but he also made me fast and when I run, I feel his pleasure". More and more Christians have come to see sport, played with the right attitude, as something that can bring pleasure to God.

No-one has said that it is easy to follow Jesus Christ in the cauldron of professional sport. There are conflicts, pressures, moral issues to be faced. In this book we shall try to identify some of those pressures and look at those who are facing them.

CHAPTER ONE

Doing the Business

In a world in which a hundredth of a second makes the difference between success and failure, is it possible to identify the characteristics which are necessary to take someone to the top? Even the phrase "the top" may need unpacking.

For one person "the top" may be being World Champion – number one in the world. For another it may be to be national champion. Thus two athletes reach the Olympic final and come fourth. One is "over the moon" about his achievement as reaching the final was the ambition; the other with a similar achievement is "gutted" not to have won a medal.

The simple answer to the question in the opening paragraph is that no one knows. If they did someone would bottle it and sell it in "Do-it-yourself Champion kits". What can we learn from the experience of a number of champions?

Ability

There is no substitute for ability, raw talent. It is something you are born with – or you aren't! It is the ability to run fast, control a racquet, hit a ball. It is good hand and eye co-ordination, fast hands and a good eye. Football manager and master of the one-liner, Tommy Docherty, once said of a footballer: "He only lacked one thing – ability". The point that he was making was that while this player had made it into the professional game the basic raw material, the natural ability to take him to the top, was not there.

Physical attributes

Size is an important factor in succeeding in sport. To state the obvious, top basketball players are tall, usually 6'6" or more. Jockeys are small. One has as much chance of being a 5'2" basketball player as a 6' jockey!

Large hands and long fingers help in sports where catching a ball is important. In some sports being left-handed is an advantage. It is interesting to note that there are many top-class left-handed cricketers, tennis players and footballers (left footed) but only one left-hander, Bob Charles, has ever reached the top in golf.

David Hemery suggests in his book *The Pursuit of Sporting Excellence: A study of sport's highest achievers* based on a series of interviews with sporting legends, "Without a fair amount of natural attributes, the competitor will not be vying for the very top." Hemery also notes that he was neither the fastest nor the strongest in the Olympic final which he won. He concludes that the "winner" in sport is perhaps the person with the highest proportion of all the necessary attributes, rather than the best at any one attribute.

Motivation

To reach the top requires motivation, single-mindedness and determination and the desire to win (see further chapter 2 on competitiveness). There must be a willingness to make the necessary sacrifices to get to the top. There is a need for self-confidence and self-belief. Unless you believe that you are going to achieve something, the chances are that you won't.

It is sometimes suggested that Christians, with their philosophy of "considering others better than themselves" (Philippians 2:3) and of esteeming their brothers better than themselves, will be out of place in the competitive world of sport. While the Christian has the promise that the meek will inherit the earth, this does not seem to apply in the world of professional sport where "the children of darkness seem wiser in their generation than the children of light".

Sport is sometimes coached in a way which urges

the player to be self-motivated and aggressive towards the opponent so that hate becomes a motivation, "the killer instinct" as its sometimes called. However, the Christian can lay hold of a different kind of motivation and realize that his talent is from God and that the expression of that talent is a celebration of what God has given him/her with the result that the motivation becomes love not hate.

Often a person will find a change of priorities resulting from becoming a Christian. Life is no longer self-centred. This changes the attitude to sport, and the motivation. However it need not affect the person's desire to win. Kriss Akabusi, the British record holder and Olympic medallist in the 400 metres hurdles, would admit to such a change of motivation. Before he became a Christian he wanted to win for himself. Now, as a Christian, his number one priority is to please God. On achieving success he is quick to give thanks to God. However the will to win remains the same.

Bernhard Langer explained his priorities to Matthew Chancellor of *Golf Weekly* shortly after he had missed the vital putt in the 1991 Ryder Cup, the golf competition between Europe and America. Had Langer's putt gone in the hole, Europe would have won the cup. "For me what matters is that I give the whole subject over to God. I just say 'If you want me to make that putt or if you want me to win this tournament then it will happen', if not then He has other plans for me."

Training

If there is no substitute for raw talent, there is equally no alternative to hard work. Talent, however great, must be exploited, developed, honed. The ball player may have great natural ability, yet will spend hours every day practising it. A willingness to put in the effort is an essential part of reaching the top. There must be a commitment, a stickability to see the job through to the end.

The average tournament golfer will warm up for an hour before playing a four-hour round. Afterwards it is back to the practice ground for another hour honing the swing followed by perhaps an hour practising one's putting.

Ed Moses, Olympic gold medallist in the 400 metres hurdles in the 1984 Olympics who, at his peak, won over 100 consecutive races is in no doubt about this aspect of the athlete's life. He says simply, "hard work got me to where I am".

Ask any professional footballer if he looks forward to pre-season training and you'll need to stand well back. For two weeks or so before the season begins players run until they drop. After the summer break pounds gained have to be shed. Weights, gym work, running laps of the pitch. Work all morning and then back for more in the afternoon.

For Lisa Opie, who won the British Open Squash Championship in 1991, the schedule of training is six days a week. In the morning she does a physical session – a long run, a series of sprints or a session of weight training. In the afternoon she plays a match.

Opportunity

Opportunity is another significant factor. If you grow up in a town without a squash court you are unlikely to become a schools squash champion! The parent of a promising teenage runner once expressed the opinion to me that it was not necessarily the best runners who won but those whose parents were able and willing to drive them all over the country to compete.

The reality is that the making of a champion involves a subtle combination of a number of factors. Take Kitrina Douglas, one of Europe's top women golfers. No one can doubt her talent. However, without application and opportunity she would never have made it to the top.

Until the age of 17 she had never held a golf club, but then spotting her talent by chance, her father suggested she take a year off and play golf full-time to see what progress she could make. The talent was there and the opportunity was provided. The rest was up to Kitrina. Through dedication and hard work she went on to become county champion in three years and to win a professional tournament within seven years.

For Lisa Opie the opportunity came with her introduction to squash by her father at the age of eleven. Her own contribution was the commitment to work at her game and to accept a life style of Friday to Sunday away playing squash which set her apart from her schoolmates and denied her a normal teenage social life. Ultimately she had to decide to leave her native Guernsey at the age of seventeen to live on the mainland in order to get more competitive squash. When she reached number two in the world and won the British Open, she knew the sacrifices had been worth it.

Luck

"Luck" may be a surprising concept to find in a Christian book. However, most sportspeople believe in luck, chance, the bounce of the ball, the rub of the green – call it what you will. It is that factor which determines whether the ball goes into the goal or hits the post and stays out, whether the cricketer is caught and out for 0 or dropped and goes on to score 100. It is being in the right place at the right time or not. It is getting the opportunity and being able to take advantage of it. An alternative view is that one makes one's own luck. In other words – that one gets what one deserves. The effort made will be rewarded accordingly.

Temperament

A hallmark of a champion is the ability to "do the business" when it matters, to serve the ace at break-point, to produce the goods in the final. This is the temperament which enables a performer to peak in the Olympic final, to win a high proportion of the crucial points in a tennis match.

There is no finer example of the champion's temperament than Kriss Akabusi. In 1992 Kriss's form was disappointing. To be honest he only ran one outstanding race all season. That race was the Olympic final! Kriss has broken the UK 400 metres hurdles record three times – first in the 1990 European Championship final (Gold Medal), then in the World Championship final in 1991 (Bronze Medal) and again in the 1992 Olympic final (Bronze medal).

In contrast Ron Clarke broke the world record (10,000 metres) repeatedly in races that didn't really matter but never won a major gold medal.

A golfer will have hit thousands of 5-iron shots to the green and will be able to do it repeatedly machine-like on the practice ground. However, on the final hole of the Open Championship, needing a four to win, suddenly hitting a 5-iron to the green is a bit more difficult. It is the player who can best play to his ability without letting the pressure get to him who becomes the champion.

Golf illustrates this point better than most sports.

If you stand on the practice ground and watch the 150 players, they all seem to strike the ball equally well. However, when the tournament gets going only a small number have any chance of winning. The determining factor is not physical – all the players are capable of striking the ball equally well. It is mental. It is the ability to be firm under pressure, to make a mistake and to cope with rather than be crushed by it.

Just prior to the 1992 UK Olympic Trials, the basis of selection for the British Athletics team for the Games, Kriss Akabusi writing in the Guardian diary summed up the significance of the event:

> On your marks ... Olympic trials, a dramatic occasion; for some a stepping stone to the ring of glory, for others the final curtain in a truncated season. The stage is set, the players are assembled, we all have to dance to the piper's tune. Four years of blood, sweat and tears all hang on the performance of this day.
>
> There is no room for error. No second chance.

Courage, perseverance and faith

Courage, the ability to cope with injury and other setbacks, is another important characteristic. Many athletes have a high pain threshold, whether natural or developed, which enables them to cope with an injury which might have laid up another person. It is the willingness to push through the pain barrier.

The words of Jesus, "No one who puts his hand to the plough and looks back is fit for service in the kingdom of God" (Luke 9:62) are as relevant to sport as to the spiritual realm. The athlete who gets to the top will be one who does not give up. There is a saying "when the going gets tough, the tough get going".

Does having a Christian faith have any relevance to success or failure in sport? Being a Christian does not give you any guarantee of success, but does it help? In the sense that knowing God is the meaning of life and gives the believer a security and a peace, a Christian faith should help in all aspects of life. However, the evidence would suggest that being a Christian neither makes you a better or worse player, nor does it give you a better or worse chance of reaching the top in sport.

The apostle Paul well understood the single-mindedness needed to succeed. Paul writes of "Forgetting what is behind and straining towards what is ahead, I press on towards the goal to win the prize for which God has called me heavenwards in Christ Jesus" (Philippians 3:13, 14). He acknowledges here the similar demands of success in sport and Christian life.

However there are several ways in which a Christian faith can affect the sportsperson. By "seeking first the Kingdom of God" (Matthew 6:33), the Christian gets life in perspective. Success in sport is therefore no longer the be-all and end-all of life. The Christian

also has in prayer a powerful weapon. This is not to
say that the Christian will be praying to win, but
rather to do God's will, to do one's best. Also Christians know that their value in life depends not on how
well they have played – whether they have won or
lost – but on their relationship with God.

Kriss Akabusi is without doubt someone who has
reached the very top in his profession. He has won
gold medals at Commonwealth, European and World
championships, Olympic silver and bronze medals
and sliced David Hemery's 22-year British record in
the 400 metres hurdles. Kriss's experience illustrates
the road to the top.

The first prerequisite for success in sport is natural
ability. No-one would question that Kriss has it.
However, it took some time to emerge. As a seven-
teen-year-old in the army he joined a colleague for a
training run and surprised the colleague by outpacing
him.

The reaction of the colleague, himself an experienced runner, was "you have got the potential to win
the army championship". Rather against Kriss's will
he was entered for an army race and won it. However,
it was not until he was well into his twenties that he
began to show signs of potential beyond club level.

Kriss had a relatively unhappy childhood, growing
up in a children's home after his parents had returned
to Nigeria. He recalls one of his earliest motivations
was related to the background. He found that people

often said when they saw him, "Oh there's the poor boy from the children's home", and he wanted to show them that he was worthwhile in his own right, that he could achieve things and did not need their sympathy.

The turning point in Kriss Akabusi's athletics career came in 1986 when he decided to switch events. At that time he was an international 400 metres runner. However, showing great realism he was able to sit down in the cold light of day and assess his position and his prospects. "I made the decision to switch to 400 metres hurdles after the European championships in Stuttgart in 1986. I looked around and realized that unless I made a move these would be my last championships. My rivals for 400 metres flat places were young. I could see the next squad coming up and I was out of it. In contrast there were no outstanding British 400 metres hurdlers."

Faced with the same evidence others would have drawn different conclusions. Some would have deluded themselves into thinking that they were better than they really were, that their prospects were OK and that they would improve. Others would be content with what had been achieved so far – the international vests, the Olympic silver medal in the relay, etc. Kriss, in contrast, had made a decision and had the determination to follow it through. He needed an intensive course in the techniques of hurdling. In the early days he regularly made a 500-mile round trip to Manchester to see a coach.

Doing the Business

Mike Whittingham, who later became Kriss's coach and who has worked with him in all his hurdling triumphs, is quoted in the biography of Kriss (*Kriss Akabusi on Track* by Ted Harrison):

> On day one when he came to see me Kriss knew exactly what he wanted. He asked me some very honest questions and I was honest with him. He said he wanted to be the best in Britain at 400 metres hurdles that year. Could he do it? What time would he run? I said that potentially he could run something fantastic. I also told him he must be prepared for a great deal of work.

Mike Whittingham's comparison of Kriss with Roger Black (whose coach he is also) is fascinating.

> Unlike Roger Black who was a Porsche from the word go, Kriss has achieved what he has achieved by dint of hard work. He has lifted himself from being a good club athlete to being an international runner by sheer effort.

Over the past few years Kriss has evolved a pattern of training in California during the early months of the year, returning to Britain in mid-May to embark on the European athletics season. He trains six days a week, a combination of roadwork, hill running and about two track sessions per week where he works both on speed and on hurdling technique.

Kriss makes an interesting distinction between different periods of the year:

> In winter I train, in the summer I practise – a
> subtle but important distinction. Three hours a day,
> six days a week. While the day is short and the
> light is short, I push my body to the limits. One
> more repetition . . . just a little faster. April 21st,
> the spring equinox, the scales tip, the balance
> changes. Speed, technique and lots of rest.

The competition itself is a curious combination of
excitement at the opportunity of victory and fear of
failure.

One of Kriss's greatest achievements was anchoring
the British 4×400 metres relay team to gold in the
World Championships in Tokyo in 1991. Kriss's own
account of that race is fascinating for the insight that
it gives us into the mind of the top athlete and the
thoughts going through his head. Speaking at Cosham
Baptist Church about a month after the race Kriss
summed up his feelings on the race like this.

> It's very funny, when you're out there doing your
> stuff you don't realize what effect you're having on
> the people back here. And when I came back to
> England I realized a lot of people follow you.
>
> We went to Tokyo with high hopes but things
> didn't go according to plan. Peter Elliott got
> injured, Tom McKean got knocked out, Linford
> Christie didn't get a medal. By the time the 4×400

metres came on the last day we just had three
medals, Liz McColgan a gold in the 10,000 metres
and me a bronze in the 400 metres hurdles and
Roger Black a silver in the 400.

We begin to think well maybe we can do something, we've got a few bronzes and a few silvers
and Liz McColgan got a gold and that weekend
everyone was looking forward to this 4×400. The
word was out to the Americans, these guys, these
Brits – they're ready! Well the American guys, our
country cousins, they went, "Gee man, they're not
worth bothering about, those guys, we're gonna
kick their butts. All right, OK. We're good enough
to kick the Brits' butts any day."

Well the night before the race I went to bed
thinking and praying. I shared with Roger Black.
"I can do it!" Roger says, "Kriss, you can do what?"
"I can run that last leg!" "Are you sure?" "Yeah,
yeah, yeah!" Because we realized that if we were
to get anywhere we had to put our best man first.
Roger would have to go on the first leg and we
didn't know who could run last. "Well," I said, "I
can do it." "Kriss, are you sure?" "Yeah." "OK."
Went down to the manager and he said OK. "Kriss
wants to run last leg." "Are you sure, Kriss?" "Yes,
I'm sure."

By now I was thinking, "Are you really sure?"
But I was sure. Anyway I got down there and when
you get down on track you get seats which say
which is your lane order plus your position. And

we line up and Roger sits on the first chair and the Americans are thinking, "What's happening here?" And then we go in slightly descending order and "Guess who they put last leg? – the oldest man in the team!" And Pettigrew who was their world champion in the flat 400 looks across at me as if to say "Are you sure?" ". . . don't worry, I'm sure!"

OK so we get down on the track and the gun goes off and Roger runs down there and . . . a great leg and puts us first and Derek Redmond goes out and runs great and John Regis goes third and guess what – I'm sitting there last and John Regis, 14 stone of pure British beef, coming at me. Yes, I'm sure, I'm sure! I get the baton and I'm off. I charged round the bend after Pettigrew and all of a sudden I come off Pettigrew's shoulder. I'm thinking, "Stay there, stay there. . ." All I see before me is a little bald head. All of a sudden I'm feeling, "Wow this thing's easy, yeah". So, round that bend and coming to the home straight. I see this home straight and I think "OK, I'm it" and I start flying past him, yeah. Oh man. And all of a sudden I'm getting about ten metres from the line and all of a sudden I hear (pants) and I think, "Oh no please God help me now so I cross that line." And I'm so relieved. . . . . . . Fantastic, we crossed the line first. We'd won. What a terrific feeling.

Here we can see the differing, even conflicting, emotions which Kriss faced on his way to the ultimate triumph – the fear, the responsibility, the courage, the joy. But even then, few of the millions of TV viewers would have any idea about the hours of blood, tears, toil and sweat on the training track to put him in condition to make that one supreme effort on the day that mattered.

Success in sport is a subtle combination of factors – ability, motivation, determination, will to win, opportunity and so on. Having reviewed the evidence and looked at some examples of successful sportspeople, perhaps we are somewhat closer to understanding the phenomenon of a champion.

CHAPTER TWO

Playing to Win

The name of the game is "win". Or as Vince Lombardi's often quoted proclamation has it, "Winning isn't everything – it's the only thing." In American sports where there has to be a winner by sudden death, shoot-out or whatever means, there is even a saying "a tie is like kissing your sister".

What makes a winner? David Hemery in *Sporting Excellence* suggests that competitiveness is "the key to the greatest difference between those who play for fun and those who must achieve". 92 per cent of the champions asked said that they challenged themselves.

The book gives an example of Seb Coe taking part in a relay race during a routine training session at his athletics club and running himself to the point of exhaustion just to win:

> The level of competitiveness bore no relation to the lack of importance of the occasion. You just had to do it.

Much of the pressure in sport at the top level is self-imposed. It relates to fulfilling the goals that you have set yourself. At the level of equal physical talent, the one who wants to win most will win. Put differently, it is the one who can least face defeat.

In this respect sport is unlike any other field of achievement. If you were to be asked to say who is the world's greatest singer, you might say Carreras or you might say Pavarotti. Either way, your choice does not denigrate the other. In sport, however, there is only one winner. To quote the Yorkshire saying, "You get nowt for coming second."

In the 1991–92 football season, Manchester United came second in the English first division. It was the club's best performance for years in the league. However, having topped the league table for most of the season, United's attitude was one of devastation and failure, not satisfaction at a good achievement. Certainly that was the view of fans of other clubs, who in the year that the Duchess of York separated from her husband, taunted United's manager with "Even Sarah Ferguson's lost her title!" In years to come, the record books will show Leeds as champions. Who will remember who was second?

That people only notice the winner is well illustrated by one of the classic moments in sports commentary, as always involving David Coleman. In the 1968 Olympic 400 metres hurdles final, as David Hemery took the gold medal by a large margin, Coleman said "Hemery first, Hennige second, who cares who's third?" A few seconds later he added rather sheepishly, "Actually it was John Sherwood of Britain who was third!"

While it is true that people remember who won the gold medal but not the runner-up, there is more to the issue than that. There is another sense in which it is not true that you get "nowt for coming second". You get an Olympic silver medal or a fat cheque, according to the occasion. Jack Nicklaus, in fact, has argued that in American professional golf you get too much for coming second. His point is that it is possible to make a good living in professional golf without ever winning a tournament. With prize money for everyone down to sixtieth place, there is no necessity to win to survive.

Competitiveness

Being competitive is an essential ingredient of any successful athlete. Steve Cram, for example, admits to timing himself driving to training each day, to see if he can beat yesterday's time!

Heather McKay, fifteen times British Open squash champion, used a practice routine of hitting the ball off the front and side walls in a figure of eight. Her record was ninety-nine consecutive hits. She still uses this exercise and still counts!

Goal-setting is an important part of this. Bernhard Langer charted his progress in golf against a series of goals. At first he wanted just to be the best golfer in

Germany. The next goal was to survive on the European tour, by finishing in the top sixty. As this was achieved the next goal was to finish in the top ten in Europe and then to be number one in Europe. Then he wanted to be successful in America and so on.

An important factor in Margaret Court's decision to retire from tennis was that she had fulfilled her ambitions. "Once I'd got the Grand Slam in 1970, I had a baby and then the goal was to get back to number one in the world. After that I was running out of goals. I could have gone on playing for the money but my heart wasn't there any more so I knew it was time to stop."

Competitiveness is that determination not to give up until the game is lost. It is the golfer holing the vital putt to stay in the match, the tennis player coming back from love-forty on sheer determination and will to win. It used to be said of the successful Liverpool football team that they were at their most dangerous when they had just conceded a goal, so strong was their determination to get back at the opponents who had dared to score. Competititon is good in that it helps people bring out their best; it focuses their energies.

Competitiveness can of course be taken too far as Brian Aitken has commented:

> Drug abuse; the taking of bennies before and tranquillizers after the game; excessive commercialization, the buying and selling of players in a fashion

reminiscent of a cattle auction; the spectre of violence, the brutal intimidation of an often superiorly skilled oppponent – all have been prompted by the increased pressure to win an ultimate victory. Even the increased technologicalization of sport can be interpreted in the same light. Cheating is condoned and violence is tolerated if the goal is victory.[1]

The killer instinct

The overwhelming desire to win is sometimes called "the killer instinct", the desire to go beyond just playing well to press home the victory by "killing-off" the opponent. This approach to sport can lead to a ruthlessness, to a win-at-all-costs philosophy. It often involves an aggressive attitude towards one's opponent, hating the opponent.

Beisser defined the "killer instinct" as that which enables a player "relentlessly and without inner prohibition or a sense of guilt to keep the pressure on his opponent while achieving victory". It is widely believed to be indispensable for athletic success. Beisser also observed how a top (unnamed) tennis player on seeing who his next opponent would be, would "undergo a strong personality change toward that opponent. He would avoid his opponent and not speak to him." In this example the preparation for the match involved acts and attitudes of aggression towards the opponent.

In an analysis of winning and losing attitudes among athletes, sport psychologist Bruce Ogilvie reported:

> Almost every truly great athlete we have interviewed during the last four years representing every major sport has consistently emphasized that in order to be a winner you must retain the killer instinct.

This involves going beyond the legitimate desire to win. It is a win-at-all-costs attitude. It is in many cases cheating, a subject which is explored elsewhere in this book.

Andy Haden, New Zealand rugby international, summed up the All Black philosophy: "I think your job on the rugby field is to win. Choose to win or choose not to play. Do everything within your power to win. Some people say we won't do that because it isn't sporting. I don't think that attitude has any place in international rugby."

That great competitor, Jimmy Connors, who even into his forties could out-battle younger opponents, sums up his attitude on court: "Maybe my methods aren't socially acceptable to some, but it's what I have to do to survive. I don't go out there to love my enemy, I go out there to squash him."

Brian Clough, manager of Nottingham Forest, expressed the sentiments well at a time when Forest were bottom of the league and without a win, in saying "If it meant getting three points on Saturday, I would shoot my grandmother. Not nastily, I would just hurt her. That is how it gets to me." Chuck Colson, White House aide to Richard Nixon in the 60s, was quoted as saying that he would run over his grandmother to get Richard Nixon elected. Several little old ladies were soon appearing on television, claiming to be Colson's grandmother and urging people to vote for the other candidate!

Bob Cousy, a top American basketball player in the 50s and 60s, called his autobiography *The Killer Instinct*. He wrote:

> The killer instinct has brought me success as a player and as a coach but it also tempted me to run over people, to break the rules, to neglect my family . . . I am no longer proud of the killer instinct.

Paul and Sue Whetnall had an unusual encounter in the 1970 Commonwealth Games. They both played in the badminton mixed doubles competition but with different partners and met in the final. As Paul – who won – says, the secret is to try to forget that your opponent is also your wife!

The Christian view

It is in the area of competitiveness that the biggest conflicts in sport are seen for the Christian. In a world where dog eats dog, how can the Christian love his neighbour as himself? The American footballer who turns the other cheek is likely to have it ground into the mud. When Jesus said "Blessed are the meek", did he know anything of the world of professional sport?

The issue, put simply, is this. If professional sportspeople become Christians, can they continue to be competitive or do they become soft? Coaches worry that their athlete will lose the ruthless streak which is necessary to take you to the top. It is true that when you become a Christian your value system changes.

Graham Daniels illustrates the point with a lighthearted story from his time as a Cambridge United player. "When I had just become a Christian and was still playing professional football, we were doing an exercise at the end of training. The players each in turn took a shot at goal. If you scored you were finished, if you missed you had to do it again until you scored. Everyone was pushing in to get to the front of the queue and I was keeping out of it. After a bit the coach said, 'Blodwyn [my nickname], you haven't had a shot for a long time, what's up?' I replied, 'Just waiting my turn, boss.' He sneered back, 'Blessed are the meek!'"

"I now think", Graham adds, "that I was wrong not to stand up for myself, not to stop people pushing in. Christians are to be meek, but not doormats."

The reverse view is given by Fritz Petersen, a member of the Baseball Chapel in the Chicago area, quoted by Carol Flake in *Spirit of Winning*:

More Than Champions

If Jesus Christ was sliding into second base, he would knock the second baseman into left field to break up the double play. Christ might not throw a spitball but he would play hard within the rules.

Tennis player Nancy Richey became a Christian late in her career. She admits that she found it increasingly difficult to reconcile her competitive emotions with her new-found Christian faith. "When I stepped on to the court I felt I was in an isolated area and the Lord was outside of that area. I knew hating my opponent was not a Christian view."

The problem here is perhaps not a conflict between the Christian and the secular but within Nancy Richey's own approach to tennis, namely that her motivation to win was based on hating her opponent.

However, Richey is far from alone in struggling with this problem. Many struggle to achieve a balance, to temper competitive enthusiasm with just the right amount of spiritual grace, while team owners and sports reporters are concerned that players who take their religion so seriously as to dampen their "killer instinct" may jeopardize the team.

But why do people only ask this about sportspeople? The issue applies just as much in business. The Christian businessman faces the same dilemmas about integrity in a competitive environment. The Christian is called to run his business with integrity, to "love his neighbour as himself" in his relationship with employees and competitors. Yet somehow the question is asked more about sportspeople than businessmen, politicians, etc.

In the macho world of male team-sports people are sometimes expected to show their aggression and competitiveness in particular ways. Alan West played professional football for nearly twenty years. Midway through his career he became a Christian. Alan was accused by his manager, who had played with him before he was a Christian, of having lost his competitiveness. "I want to hear you swearing at the opposition, the way you used to," the manager said. Alan tried to explain that he was as keen to win as ever and didn't need to swear to prove it but he wasn't sure that the manager was convinced.

Tom Landry, a top American football coach, made this distinction: "If you say you can't play within the rules and play a tough punishing type of game, you can't play as a Christian. You try to eliminate the vicious side of the game but you have to punish the opposition." Hard but fair in a nutshell, but where do you draw the line?

Kriss Akabusi has an interesting perspective on the dichotomy between sport and faith.

I am that dichotomy. The saying is that Jesus preached a social gospel: love others more than oneself; while sport preaches the selfish: I love me, who do you love? . . . Sportsmen can easily become disillusioned with what the glamour life has to offer. Vanity, pure vanity, if this is all there is. No, Christians in sport is not two diametrically opposing ideologies but rather the realization that the talent one has is a gift from God for the benefit of society in the furtherance of the Gospel, while personally enjoying the spin-offs.

Biblical view

What does the Bible say that might be of relevance to this question? The full quotation that we referred to above is "Blessed are the meek for they will inherit the earth" (Matthew 5:5). Meekness is not easy to define. It is an attitude of patient submission and humility. Meekness for the Christian in an acceptance of adversity, knowing that God is in control of life.

Bishop David Jenkins comments helpfully:

Meekness is taken today to be a quality of the weak. The meek are the passive, the spineless, those born to be put upon, nature's doormats. . . Meekness in the seventeenth century was a quality of strength and the word used is better translated as the New English Bible does, "those of gentle spirit". An appropriate picture to have in interpreting this beatitude is that of the gentle giant, a large heavy athlete, who wants to win the confidence and inspire the affection and obtain the co-operation of a timid little girl. He lowers his voice and carefully controls his cumbersome movements, perhaps even getting down on his knees, so that he can allay her fears and make it easy for her to communicate with him. When he can make her see that his strength is under the control of his gentle will and that all he wants to do is to help her and enjoy her company, then the strength becomes a reassurance not a threat.

The fruit of the Spirit (Galatians 5:22, 23) includes "gentleness". In dealing with a problem in the church at Corinth, Paul writes: "By the meekness and gentleness of Christ, I appeal to you" (2 Corinthians 10:1). Again he writes to the Ephesians: "Be completely humble and gentle" (Ephesians 4:2) and to the Philippians: "Do nothing out of selfish ambition or vain conceit but in humility consider others better than yourselves. Each of you should look not only to your own interests, but also to the interests of others" (Philippians 2:3–4).

The application of Matthew 20:16: "The last will be first and the first will be last", to the world of sport is less clear!

There is no doubt that humility, meekness, gentleness are essential parts of the Christian character but we still have to work out how it affects our attitude to competitive sport. It seems that these verses tell us more about how we should conduct ourselves in the heat of the battle and in any other sphere of our Christian life, than about whether or not we can compete to win. As Christians we are to act with

meekness and gentleness in our relationships with
others. We are not to be arrogant or boastful. Meekness too has to be understood. Was Jesus the "Gentle
Jesus, meek and mild" of the hymn? I doubt if the
Pharisees or money-changers thought so.

For some Christians, however, this is a very difficult area. They find it hard to be competitive without
feeling that they are compromising their faith. For
some it is hard to make the association between sport
and Christianity. However in our view there is no
reason why we cannot compete to win and give it 100
per cent without any conflict with our faith. Despite
the difficulty, we believe that it can be done. Moreover because of the great potential for the Christian
to be a witness in and through sport, we would go
further and say it should be done.

As Paul told the Colossians: "Whatever you do,
work at it with all your heart, as working for the Lord"
(Colossians 3:23). The justification for being involved
in the world of sport, if one is needed, can also be
found in the Great Commission, the command of
Jesus to "go and make disciples of all nations"
(Matthew 28:19).

Witness

In a situation where being competitive is the order
of the day, where everyone is concentrating on looking after their own interests, an alternative life style

can be deeply challenging to those around.

When Cambridge United signed Alan Comfort, a left-winger from Queen's Park Rangers, the writing was rather on the wall for Graham Daniels, Cambridge United's current left-winger.

Alan was not unnaturally a little wary of Graham, wondering how he would react to the new player who was threatening his livelihood. As time progressed Alan began to notice that

there was something different about him that I couldn't quite understand. His contract was up, his wife was expecting their first child, he was out of the team. Nothing seemed to be going right for him, yet there was something special about him I couldn't really understand. He had something that I didn't have.

In contrast, I had everything that I wanted. I had signed a really good contract, I was in the team, I thought I had made it, and yet I felt really empty. I thought it was material things that made you happy in life and I had them. He didn't and yet he had a happiness that I didn't. I had never seen anyone with so much security. He knew exactly where he was going. I watched him from a distance, trying to work it all out in my own mind, exactly what was going on.

In the end I decided I had to find out for myself. I started talking to him and eventually I plucked up the courage to go to church with him.

The end of the story is that Alan became a Christian. His interest in Christianity, however, was first aroused by the quality of life of his team-mate Graham Daniels.

Another example of Christian faith expressed in a practical way involves Nduka Odizor, a quarter-finalist at Wimbledon in the early 80s. "The Duke" takes up the story.

> I was playing the qualifying round of a grass tournament in Holland when I noticed my next opponent was upset about something. I overheard him say that he had been unable to get a pair of grass-court shoes and as a result he was slipping all over the place. I offered to lend him a pair of mine.

> My opponent's face dropped in astonishment. The thought "How could anyone be so stupid?" was written all over his face.

> "Here's my hotel key", I said, "if you want to go and get them or send someone for them."

> When our match was called, there he was wearing my shoes. He won the first set, but I came back to win the next two. At the end he couldn't say thank you enough. He was so sincere. Nothing like this had ever happened to him before.

Contrast this with the player described earlier whose preparation for a match required him to avoid speaking to his next opponent.

When Phil Starbuck became a Christian he was playing for Nottingham Forest. Initially he had found

it very difficult to tell the other players. He had
prayed with the elders of his church about it. They
told him that God's timing was perfect and that he
would create the opportunity.

Then one day, quite soon after, he was getting
changed for training when the Forest captain, Stuart
Pearce, shouted across a crowded changing room,
"Hey, Starby, what's this about you getting all
religious?"

Phil's instant reaction was, "Ah, this must be the
perfect timing they were talking about!" At first he
wanted the ground to swallow him, but then he
thought "Go for it, Phil", and told them what had
happened in his life.

Alan West had a similar experience when he was
playing for Luton Town. He had become a Christian
during the summer break. The difficult bit was how
to tell the players. He prayed about it. One day, after
training, the players were in the communal bath when
a voice piped up, "Hey, Westie. You're different.
You've stopped swearing. What is it about you?"
Alan's reaction was "Oh no, Lord – not in the bath!"

There seems no reason why the Christian need
aspire to no more than being a lovable and gracious
loser. Paul's teaching about doing whatever you do
with all your heart applies. Thus when Christians find
themselves in contention for a major prize there is
no reason why they should not be as determined to
win as anyone else.

CHAPTER THREE

Winning at all Costs

With the stakes so high, it is inevitable that cheating raises its ugly head. In the history of sport there have been the celebrated cases of cheating, like Boris Onashenko, the Russian Olympic fencer who managed to wire up his equipment so that he appeared to be scoring points when he wasn't. He was rumbled and sent home in disgrace.

There have been many instances of cheating or alleged cheating in marathon races with runners taking a short cut, having someone else run half the race for them, even travelling by car for part of the way! Even the apostle Paul was aware of the possibility of cheating when he wrote to Timothy:

> Similarly, if anyone competes as an athlete, he does not receive the victor's crown unless he competes according to the rules.
>
> 2 Timothy 2:5

Definition

The dictionary definition of cheating, "to deceive or defraud", is not entirely helpful. A better definition might refer to gaining an unfair advantage but then who is to decide what is fair and what is not? Kriss Akabusi suggests "anything which is outside the boundaries of the law of the land or the sport".

Denis Norden once suggested the following conjugation of the verb to be a bore: "I am not a bore, you are a bore, he is a bore, she is a bore, etc". Similarly there are those who might conjugate the verb to cheat: "I take advantage of the rules, you cheat. . ." It was Maradona's "hand of God" handball which eliminated England from the 1986 World Cup. [See p. 68] Would we have risen in such a vehement protest for justice if the incident had gone in our favour rather than against England? In the eyes of the partisan supporter, the same tackle can be nasty and vicious when against our team and clumsy or unlucky if committed by our team.

David Hemery identifies what he calls "four levels of gamesmanship":

1. Activities which "could not under any circumstances be regarded as breaking the rules".
2. Conning the referee.
3. The professional foul.
4. Intention of ending a player's career.

It may be helpful to discuss each of these in turn.

Using the rules

What Hemery refers to as "activities which could not under any circumstances be regarded as breaking the rules" could also be called "using the rules". It is using the rules of the sport to your advantage. One aspect of this is what one might call legitimate deception. These, by anyone's standards, are acceptable behaviour.

Think, for example, of the footballer who sells the opponent a dummy (by feigning right and then going left) or of the cricket fielder who moves slowly in order to persuade the batsman that there is time to take a second run, then pounces like a flash and runs him out.

In rugby union it has traditionally been a common ploy for the scrum half to pretend that the ball has come out of the scrum and to pretend to pass it in order to catch the opposition offside as they chase what they assume to be the ball. It has been argued that the scrum half is guilty of gamesmanship in that the sole purpose of his ruse is to try to gain a penalty for his team. It can equally be argued that it is the team caught offside that is the one guilty of "cheating" by not waiting until they are sure that the ball is in play. This might be seen to be a grey area. [The administrators obviously think so as the dummy was made illegal in 1992.]

Another example of this might be playing quickly/

slowly to upset the preferred tempo of the opponent. A golfer who knows that his opponent likes to play slowly, at a measured pace, might play at breakneck speed in order to put pressure on his opponent to play more quickly than he/she wants to.

Certain tennis players and golfers have been accused of using the referee as a ploy. The player is entitled to call for the referee to settle a point of dispute or give an interpretation of the laws. As such, calling the referee cannot be deemed to be cheating. However if a player calls for the referee when the opponent is "on a roll", in order to cause a delay in play which will stop the opponent's momentum and give himself time to regroup, is that at least gamesmanship?

Another grey area would be attempts to gain a psychological advantage. Examples would include going up to an opponent who has just recovered from an injury before a game and saying, "How's your shoulder? I hope it won't affect you today." Former Olympic swimming gold medallist, Duncan Goodhew, tells of opponents who would come across to shake hands after the starter had called them to their blocks. While no-one could call a handshake cheating, Goodhew felt that the timing made it an attempt to break his concentration and started to react aggressively to it.

Monica Seles's habit of grunting as she hits the ball caused quite a stir amongs tennis administrators. Was she grunting to gain an advantage? Was it within the rules? At what decibel level can a grunt be deemed to put off an opponent? There are no easy answers.

Nick Faldo was playing Graham Marsh of Australia in the World Matchplay Championship at Wentworth one year. Faldo's approach to the sixteenth green was too strong and went through the green. Seconds later the ball changed direction, finished up on the green quite close to the flag. While no-one had actually seen what happened, there is little doubt that a patriotic supporter had picked the ball up and had thrown it on to the green to improve Faldo's chance. Faldo arrived at the green with his ball in a much better position than it deserved. He putted out, halved the hole and went on to win the match.

He had done nothing wrong, he had broken no rule, as no-one had seen the ball being thrown it could not be proved that it had not struck a spectator and bounced on to the green. In any case Faldo had not asked a spectator to kick his ball on to the green so why should he be penalized? Nevertheless, afterwards he was criticized for acting in an unsporting manner by some who felt that he should have conceded the hole in the interests of fair play.

The final of the 10,000 metres race in the 1992 Olympics ended in controversy. As the race neared its completion a Moroccan runner, Khalid Skah, and Richard Chelimo were clear on their own. As they prepared to lap another Moroccan runner, Hammou Boutayeb, the latter, rather than allowing himself to be lapped, continued to run with the other two.

The rules state that "pacing in races by runners

lapped or about to be lapped" is forbidden. Officials decided that Skah's victory had been assisted by Boutayeb's intervention and Skah was accordingly disqualified.

Next day, following a protest by the Moroccan team management, the jury of appeal reinstated Skah as winner declaring there had been no contravention of the rules by that runner. Skah had claimed that he had told Boutayeb to go away and not to make problems for him. Boutayeb said that he was doing no more than trying to defend his honour by preventing a fellow Moroccan from lapping him.

Athletics Today, in its Olympic report, began its account of the 10,000 metres in fairly emotive language.

> The arguments will continue to rage: did Khalid Skah cheat his way to the Olympic 10,000 metres crown? Or was the intervention by the lapped runner, fellow Moroccan Hammou Boutayeb, quite unplanned?

In the end the point at issue seemed to be that it was necessary to prove intent and no-one was able to do that.

A question arises about whether or not some of these practices might be regarded as gamesmanship. When does using legitimate means to gain a psychological advantage become gamesmanship? Even if these practices could not "under any circumstances be regarded as breaking the rules", are they against the "spirit of the law" – if such a thing exists? We will return to that issue later.

Conning the referee

This category is without doubt cheating. This is where a player deliberately breaks the rules of the game in order to gain advantage or attempts to deceive the referee/umpire.

Examples of this would include a tennis/squash player playing the ball after the second bounce but claiming that it was in play, a golfer improving the lie of the ball or even dropping a replacement ball and playing it as if the original ball was being played where it lay, a cricketer claiming a catch when he knows the ball hasn't carried to him.

Probably the most famous example of cheating occurred during the quarter-final of the football World Cup in Mexico in 1986. During the match between England and Argentina the score was 0–0 when Diego Maradona chased a high through ball. Unable to reach the ball with his head he stuck up his hand and punched the ball past England's goalkeeper Peter Shilton. There was no doubt that he used his hand but in the heat of the moment the referee did not see it properly and gave the goal. Afterwards Maradona referred to a goal by "the hand of God".

How do professional players react to an incident like this? Glenn Hoddle played for England that day.

In his book *Spurred to Success* he wrote of the incident:

> I know what I felt about the incident then and I feel the same way now . . . I saw Maradona punch the ball in . . . he tried to disguise it very well flicking his head at the same time. But it hadn't fooled me . . . I had seen it done in Sunday morning matches at the local park and the players there have never got away with it. But in Mexico, in a World Cup quarter-final, here was an official who shouldn't have been trusted even with a Sunday morning match. I don't blame Diego Maradona, I blame the Tunisian referee, Ali Bennaceur. I saw the referee look over to the linesman, turn and blow his whistle and point to the centre circle, indicating a goal.
>
> I felt absolutely sick inside. I chased after him. . . I pointed to my hand screaming "handball". It was at this moment I knew with a sickening feeling in my guts that the referee hadn't seen it. . . The horrible image of Maradona handling the ball will always remain with me. The nauseating feeling of knowing that you have been cheated won't go away either. . . It was wrong. England should never have been beaten by a goal like that.

While Hoddle's comments on the referee are totally justified, it is astonishing that he can say, "I don't blame Maradona".

Other examples of trying to con the referee by

shouting "our ball" when they know that they have hit it out, or diving in the penalty area in the hope of gaining a free-kick or a penalty are also common.

During the 1990 World Cup the German team was accused more than once of feigning injuries to try to con the referee. Gordon Durie of Tottenham Hotspur was found guilty of misconduct in exactly these circumstances and banned for three matches in October 1992. After a flare-up with a Coventry City player, Durie suddenly fell backwards and lay motionless on the pitch. After studying video evidence, the FA Disciplinary Commission decided that Durie was guilty of feigning injury but later acquitted on appeal.

Another example of cynical (and in this case premeditated) cheating occurred during a rugby international between Wales and New Zealand in 1978. With just minutes remaining Wales led 10–9 but New Zealand gained a line-out.

As the ball was thrown in two New Zealand players – Andy Haden and Frank Oliver – dived out of the line-out as if they had been pushed. The referee was conned, a penalty was awarded and New Zealand won the match 12–10.

In his autobiography called *Captain*, Graham Mourie, who played for New Zealand in the match, said that they had decided in advance to use that tactic if they needed to.

An altogether more difficult issue to consider is "walking" in cricket. According to the laws of cricket it is the umpire who decides if a batsman is out.

However a tradition has grown up in the game that when a player knows he has hit the ball and is caught, he "walks" (i.e. he gives himself out and walks off the pitch without waiting for the umpire's decision).

This situation usually occurs when a batsman edges the ball to the wicket keeper or is caught off bat and pad. Often in such situations only the batsman knows if the ball hit his bat or only his pad, arm, etc.

While it is "sporting" to walk, the batsman who waits for the umpire's decision cannot be said to cheat – he is following the letter of the law. Yet in many cricketing circles staying (and not walking) when you know that you are out is regarded as cheating.

It seems to be quite common for players to adopt double standards or situational ethics on this issue. The author has heard Ian Botham, Fred Trueman and Alan Knott say that while they would normally walk when they knew they were out, there were circumstances when they would not. Australians generally do not walk. The three players argue that if you walk in a match in which the opposition are not walking, then you give them an advantage.

A further dimension of this issue is the player who usually walks and has such a reputation. If in an important match that player nicks the ball but does not walk, the umpire may be influenced by his reputation for walking and assume that as he has not walked he must not have hit the ball. In this way a player can be honest most of the time, but be dishonest when he really needs it!

One hears of teams which do their homework on the referee and include in the team-talk an assessment of him. The players are told what to expect from the referee, what issues the referee enforces strictly and areas where he is likely to be less strict. The aim is that the team should "play to the referee" and exploit any weaknesses to their advantage. Is this gamesmanship or is it just using the rules and the referee's interpretation of them?

The professional foul

The so-called professional foul is the situation where a player (usually in football) has a clear opportunity to score with only the goalkeeper to beat. A defender with no legitimate means of preventing the opponent from scoring fouls him – by tripping him, pulling him back, rugby tackling him, etc. An alternative scenerio is when the defender deliberately handles the ball to prevent a goal-scoring opportunity.

This problem in professional football has been largely overcome by the decision of the governing body, FIFA, that a player who commits a professional foul on a player in a goal-scoring position shall be sent off the field. There is, however, still the element of judgement by the referee as to whether or not the player fouled was in a goal-scoring position as opposed to just an attacking position.

However, the attitude of the professional player to

the professional foul is of considerable interest. Bryan Robson, for several years Manchester United and England captain, is quoted in Hemery's book on the subject.

> In open play I don't think I'd use gamesmanship but if someone went through with just a goalkeeper to beat and I could catch him by bringing him down, I'd bring him down. If I didn't I'd feel I'd let my team-mates and my fans down. . . I've never been a player where the ref's back's turned, that I'd kick someone or elbow someone, because they are to get an advantage on me. I'd never do that.

It is an interesting paradox that Robson can say that he would not use gamesmanship, but felt that the professional foul was not only a legitimate weapon in a given situation but also his responsibility. There is no doubt that the motivation not to let the team down is a strong motivating factor in all team sports. It should also be noted that Robson's comments are from an era prior to the introduction of the automatic sending-off for a professional foul.

The FIFA ruling that a player who commits a foul which deprives an opponent of a goal-scoring opportunity must be sent off is not without controversy. Many people in the game would like referees to be given some discretion. As those well-known football pundits, Gilbert and Sullivan, would put it, it is all a question of making the punishment fit the crime.

In the 1980 FA Cup Final, Martin Allen of West

Ham United got clear of the Arsenal defence. Willie Young, who was chasing him, tripped him just outside the penalty area. A free kick resulted, much less of a goal-scoring opportunity than had Allen been allowed to continue. Under the prevailing code of discipline, Young was cautioned by the referee but not sent off. His "cheating" had paid off.

Whether it is fair to call Young's actions "cheating" is a moot point. Dick Farr played hockey for Cambridge, Exeter University, British Universities, England Under 21 and Hampstead as a goalkeeper. (He is now an Anglican vicar, a guardian of moral values.) Dick regarded bringing down an opponent to deny a goal-scoring opportunity and taking his chance with the penalty kick as quite legitimate.

> The rules allow for it. I am accepting the rules of the game. There is nothing underhand about it. I am taking a particular action – bringing down an opponent – and accepting the consequences. If the consequences include being sent off and leaving the team a player short, then one has to think harder about it than when I was playing hockey. I would not regard this as cheating. Conning the umpire, feigning an injury to get someone sent off, that is cheating – deliberately conceding a penalty is not cheating, it is playing within the framework of the rules.

Brian Irvine is a Christian who plays in the back four

for Aberdeen and has played for Scotland. It is his job to stop the opposition from scoring. How does he see the line between the legitimate and the deliberate foul?

> The FIFA ruling that a deliberate foul on a player in a goal-scoring position results in an automatic sending-off has made it easier in a way. Also in the Scottish League, even before the FIFA ruling, referees usually took that line anyway.
>
> The hardest thing for me is when I'm marking a really good player and I'm told to clobber him early in the game. I am quite prepared to get in a hard tackle as soon as I can, to show him that I'm there, but I couldn't go out and just kick somebody.

Last year Brian was involved in an incident, which is amusing in retrospect, but was anything but it at the time. Playing for Aberdeen in a Scottish League match, Brian made a tackle in the penalty area. The forward went down and the referee awarded a penalty. Goalkeeper Theo Snelders was so incensed by the decision that his protests ended in his being sent off. Brian Irvine, who had conceded the penalty, found himself putting on the goalkeeper's jersey. He saved the penalty too.

Attempting to end another player's career

While Hemery includes this fourth category in his book and states that anyone guilty of it should be banned from all future participation in sport and regarded as a criminal, he has encountered no documented cases of it.

In a game against Canterbury on the 1971 British Lions tour of New Zealand, three Lions players were taken off injured. As the Lions were winning the test series the Lions wondered if the injuries were just coincidence or if it was part of a calculated plan to take certain key Lions players out of the next Test.

John Jackson of the Pittsburgh Steelers American football team, asked whether he regarded trying to injure the opposition quarterback during a game as a legitimate ploy, replied, "I don't think it's part of people's game plan but it doesn't hurt when there's a quality quarterback there if you get him out of the game." The trouble is that in American football a certain level of violence is part of the game. That makes it difficult to know where to draw the line.

Sportsmanship

But where is sportsmanship in all this? Is the concept of fair play and playing the game an unrealistic notion in the world of competitive sport? Has sportsmanship and the sense of goodwill in playing the game been sacrificed totally to an obsession with winning?

The Central Council for Physical Recreation recently launched an initiative called "Fair Play in Sport" with an appeal to

> people who still passionately support the British concepts of good sportsmanship and fair play, who would like to see a concerted effort made to encourage a return to the standards that made British sport the envy of the world.

The charter called upon competitors to:

— abide by the laws and spirit of the sport;
— accept the decisions of the referee without question;
— not to cheat or use performance-enhancing drugs;
— exercise self-control at all times;
— accept success and failure with good grace;
— treat opponents with respect.

The Council of Europe (7th conference of European Ministers responsible for sport, May 1992) went even further, arguing not only that "ethical considerations leading to fair play are integral and not optional elements of all sports activity" but also that participants in sport had "a responsibility to behave in a way which sets a good example and presents a positive role model for children and young people".

The whole notion of sportsmanship was considered in a 1992 BBC Television programme in the *More Than a Game* series. The programme gave two illustrations of sportsmanship at the top level. In 1964 the British two-man bob (bobsleigh) team of Robin Dixon and Tony Nash were in contention for the gold medal. After the first of their two runs, the British pair discovered that the main bolt holding their back axle in place had snapped in half. There would be no time to have a replacement brought.

The British pair's main rival, Eugenio Monte of Italy, the current world champion, on hearing of the Britons' plight, removed the bolt from his own bob after his second run, to have it fitted in the British bob. The Britons won the gold medal. As Robin Dixon of the British team pointed out, "Monte knew that he was sacrificing his chance of an Olympic gold medal, the only significant prize that he had not won, by his action."

Monte's comment on the incident was, "My action was very normal for a sportsperson. You try to help the other people to have the same conditions that you have." Eugenio still has the mug presented to him by the British team with the inscription: "A great sporting gesture". Whether or not such a gesture would happen today with the greater commercial pressure and obsession with winning is very doubtful.

The programme also used a comparison of the same

incident in two games fifty years apart to show how attitudes had changed. In 1940 Dartmouth played Cornell. In American football a team has four attempts to attack (four downs) and then possession is lost. Dartmouth led 3–0 in the last seconds. Cornell failed to score in any of their four downs. The referee, who had miscounted, awarded a fifth down from which Cornell scored to win the match.

On learning afterwards of the circumstances of their victory, Cornell conceded the game to Dartmouth. As one of their players said, "There was no point in keeping the game. They had won it fairly. Right was right, they should have the game back. Fair is fair. It's not whether you win but how you play the game that matters."

Fifty years on and the Colorado Buffalos play the Missouri Tigers in another college match. Again the referee awarded a fifth down with two seconds of play remaining. Colorado scored and clinched the game. On this occasion there was no question of Colorado doing anything but "riding their luck".

Bill McCartney, the football coach of the University of Colorado, said:

It just so happened that we were awarded an extra down and there are a lot of people that could have called attention to it. We didn't do it knowing we were gaining an extra down. Had we known and proceeded with it I don't think we could live with ourselves, but we operated fairly. It was ten

minutes after the game before I came to an aware-
ness that we had scored on a fifth down. I have to
answer to my team. I can't answer to everybody
out there.

There's a verse in Scripture – 1 Corinthians 4:4 –
it says "my conscience is clear but that does not
make me innocent. It is the Lord who judges me."
You see only the Lord can judge a man's innermost
thoughts; only the Lord can look into a guy's heart
and see what he is clearly thinking. I do not have any
guilt attached to any decisions that we made. I felt
like we earned everything that we got and we operated within the rules as they were presented to us.

It is interesting that McCartney's "defence" starts
with his responsibility to his team, with the sugges-
tion that forfeiting the game would have let the team
down. His quotation of Scripture in this context
seemed a little bizarre.

Having said that, it is not clear exactly what "giving
the game back to the opponents" actually means. A
game is played, the referee makes the decisions, and
the final score is registered. For one team the following day to say that they concede their victory and
give it back to the opposition sounds good in theory
but does not seem very practical in any competitive
sports situation.

Most professional sportspeople would probably
regard a defeat in these circumstances as just one of
those things which happen, which next time would

probably go in one's favour rather than to one's disadvantage. There are certainly numerous examples of a football game in which the crucial goal was offside or a turning point in a cricket match when an umpiring decision whether to give a batsman out or not out which was subsequently shown to be an incorrect decision had a significant effect on the final outcome of the game.

One of the outstanding examples of sportsmanship occurred during the 1969 Ryder Cup, the golf competition between Great Britain and America. The destiny of the Ryder Cup in 1969 depended on the last match on the last day between Jack Nicklaus and Tony Jacklin.

Both players were on the eighteenth green in two shots. Jacklin putted first leaving the ball about two to three feet short. Nicklaus charged his putt about six feet past and then holed the return which left Jacklin needing to hole his two-foot putt under enormous pressure to tie the Ryder Cup. However, Jack Nicklaus picked up Jacklin's marker, conceded the putt and offered a handshake. The match was tied.

As he walked off the green Nicklaus put his arm round Jacklin and said, "I don't think you would have missed the putt but I would never have given you the chance." Nicklaus said afterwards, "I just thought after all he had done for golf it would have been such a terrible shame if he had missed that putt and been remembered for that."

While not in any way wanting to detract from

Nicklaus's sporting action it is difficult to make comparisons between sports and to expect a similar gesture in a different sport. For one thing golf is played at walking pace with a stationary ball.

The golfer is much more in control of his own destiny than is the case in a game played at top speed with a moving ball. Moreover, the procedure for conceding a putt is an accepted part of golf. That Nicklaus conceded the putt was not in itself strange; that is part of match-play golf. What makes it special is that he did it at the crucial moment and that his concern for his opponent seemed greater than his desire to press a team victory in a situation which could have left his opponent psychologically shattered. It is difficult to think of a similar gesture which could have occurred in professional football for example.

Nonetheless Nicklaus sets out a helpful yardstick against which to judge one's behaviour:

> A man's own honour and integrity is worth more than the winning or the losing of the game. I think that's what it is. It's very important to me that I can go home at night and sleep knowing that I've played the game fair – win or lose. It's your own integrity and your own honour, that's what you play with.

Frost and Sims, (*Development of human values through sport*, 1974) gave details of another example of sportsmanship.

Ten minutes remained in the 1969 Spanish Football league championship game played before 80,000 screaming fans in the enormous Bernabeu Stadium in Madrid. With the game scoreless, Pedro Zamballa, right wing for one of the teams, skilfully manoeuvred the ball near the opponent's goal and prepared to shoot from fairly close range. Readying himself to defend Zamballa's impending shot, the goalkeeper on the other team collided with one of his own team-mates; so forcefully, in fact, that both fell to the ground injured and unconscious. Facing a defenceless goal, Zamballa could have scored easily. Instead, he did a remarkable thing. He deliberately kicked the ball wide of the goal and over the end line. Zamballa's team eventually lost the game by a score of 1–0. His refusal to score a goal may well have cost his team the championship.

Zamballa's conduct was both criticized and praised. His fans and teammates denounced his seemingly charitable act: "Zamballa is paid to shoot goals, not to make gifts to the other side," they said. "What would happen if every footballer and every athlete declined, when the fancy took him, to score or to seize a chance of winning, even if he were responding to the dictates of his conscience?" On the other hand, the International Committee on Fair Play honoured his conduct by presenting him with an award "for reflecting all that is finest and purest in sport". However, even the committee

was ambivalent, noting that Zamballa's act consti-
tuted "an extreme case of fair play".

Against the spirit of the law

This would be an activity which does not break any
individual rule but attempts to gain an advantage
which the rules are intended to prevent.

The playing conditions governing Test cricket in
England lay upon the captains the duty of adhering
not only to the letter of the law but the spirit of the
law. To do otherwise would not be cricket I suppose!

Three examples, ironically, of a practice which
while entirely legal might be said to go against the
spirit of the law come from cricket.

Qualification from the zonal stage to the quarter-
finals of cricket's Benson and Hedges Cup is determined by points (for wins and draws) and on run-rate
(runs per over) where teams were equal on points.
Somerset went into their final zonal match knowing
that a win would see them into the quarter-finals.

However defeat would also see them through provided their run-rate was maintained at its current
level. Brian Rose, the Somerset captain, decided that
trying to win the match involved the risk of seeing
their run-rate deteriorate. As a result Somerset, batting first, faced one ball and declared without scoring
a run. The opposition batted, scored one run and won
the match.

Yet by protecting their superior run-rate Somerset had gone into the quarter-final. Their actions were within the rules of the competition but were they fair or ethical?

In August 1988, my co-director of Christians in Sport, Andrew Wingfield Digby, found himself making the sporting headlines. Captaining Dorset against Cheshire in the Minor Counties, Andrew was faced with a game heading for a draw. Cheshire, chasing 201 to win, were 92–6 with 11 overs left. Andrew instructed Graeme Calway to bowl wides. He bowled 14 consecutive wide deliveries all of which were allowed to run to the boundary. By the end of the over 56 extras had been conceded as well as four runs off the bat.

Cheshire had progressed to 152–6 and suddenly the target of 201 seemed attainable. Cheshire, sensing a chance of victory, started to take risks. In the end they were all out for 183. Dorset had won. However, the matter did not end there. The Minor Counties Cricket Association introduced a new law that 10 points would be deducted for an action which could be deemed to bring the game into disrepute. The deliberate bowling of wides would be an example of this.

The other instance was when New Zealand needed 6 to win off the last ball of the match. The Australian bowler Trevor Chappell, after consultation with the captain, his brother Greg Chappell, bowled underarm, rolling the ball along the ground. Thus he made it virtually impossible for the batsman to generate the height needed to hit the ball for six runs. After the game the incident was widely condemned as unsporting and against the spirit of the laws.

There are, however, situations when the spirit of the law might be deemed to go against the letter. When the non-striker backs up (i.e. starts on a run) before the ball is bowled, the convention within the game is that the bowler gives a warning to the batsman the first time but may run him out if it recurs.

Why should this be? The batsman who backs up early is "cheating" in the sense that he is trying to gain an unfair advantage. Yet to give him his just desserts, in accordance with the laws of the game, is deemed to be unsporting. This may be partly to discourage bowlers from pretending to bowl while holding onto the ball in order to deceive the batsman in order to run him out.

Timewasting

Timewasting is one of the curses of professional football at the moment. It is to combat it that the administrators have first restricted the goalkeeper to four steps and then banned passing back to the goalkeeper.

However the problem is deeper. It is an attitude. The situation arises when a team has a lead and needs therefore to do no more to win the game than hang on. The team takes as long as possible to do everything. Players take the ball and stand by the corner flag with it. There is nothing wrong with this in itself. There is no law which says that a player may not stand by the corner flag with the ball. Yet the overall impression is of unsporting behaviour.

Violence

Violence on the field of play is another issue to be considered. In rugby a certain amount of violence is accepted. Rugby is after all a physical-contact sport. The question arises about how much is legitimate. Where does one draw the line around acceptable violence? Simon Smith who played for Wasps and England comments.

> In my experience most players go out to play rugby hard but fair. You accept the hard tackle. If you have gone down on the ball and not released it – so that you are stopping play from flowing – you would accept being kicked or raked. There is an adage in the game "Give them a good kicking and they won't do it again". Sometimes the deliberate late tackle is condoned on the grounds that if I am out of the game I might as well put my opponent out of the game as well.

Barry Morrison, vicar of St Luke's, Hampstead, played top-level rugby for several years, for London

Scottish and Bristol recalled his experience:

> My biggest problem was being obstructed in the
> line-out. Once a famous Scottish international
> opponent was guilty, and I administered "divine"
> retribution – a short, sharp blow to the solar plexus.
> He appealed to the ref, only to be told: "I know
> you and I know him. And he's a minister, and
> he wouldn't have hit you unless you had done
> something wrong."

In November 1992 Peter Marsh was jailed for two
months for inflicting grievous bodily harm on an
opponent during an amateur rugby league match.
While this is the only occurrence of a custodial sen-
tence resulting from an incident on the sports field,
there have been other cases when players have taken
legal action against an opponent.

In 1992 Gary Blissett of Brentford was acquitted at
Salisbury Crown Court of a charge of grievous bodily
harm after an incident in which his elbow smashed a
Torquay United player's cheekbone.

In cricket the issue is the bouncer, short-pitched
fast bowling which often hits the batsman. It is sometimes called "intimidatory bowling".

There is of course one sport above all others in
which violence is licensed, boxing. An article in the
Observer last year tried to understand the fascination
with boxing, a barbaric practice in our refined twenti-
eth-century society. It suggested that the enjoyment
of boxing was

the same impulse that sends sightseers flocking to somewhere like the Yorkshire Ripper's house to have their pictures taken. Trust death – actual death, public and violent, and the possibility of death, or at least bloody disfigurement and mutilation – to pull in the crowds.

Boxing promoter Barry Hearn was quoted:

Everybody likes to see the fights. The hair on the back of your neck stands up. You watch the faces in a boxing crowd when it gets exciting and you see expressions on people's faces that you don't see anywhere else. It's a different expression. Motor-racing, the crowds are always on the bends. That's in people.

The article also referred to one of the earliest televised fights, Emile Griffith – Benny "Kid" Paret world welterweight title fight in March 1962. The fight was shown live and repeated later.

The replay went on air showing the brutal beating Paret was taking and pulled in higher ratings than the fight itself; people were calling friends and telling them to tune in, that a guy was getting beaten to death on television.

(Paret died in a coma ten days later.)

Since the Second World War over 350 boxers have died from ring injuries. Defenders of boxing, however, always point out that the fatality rate in boxing is lower than in many other sports. American football is allegedly more dangerous and it is claimed that a higher proportion of jockeys are killed.

Just how violent boxing can be is illustrated by the following three quotations from people on the inside.

I try to catch my opponent on the tip of his nose because I try to punch the bone into his brain.

> Mike Tyson, former world
> heavyweight champion

The job requires a man to move toward a battered, beaten foe whose hands are down, whose eyes are rolling and, if the referee allows, smash his face again.
> Muhammad Ali's biographer,
> Thomas Hauser

The objective is to incapacitate your man and they [the crowd] want to see you do it. They want to see it done to you, or you do it to the man. But they want to see it. They don't really care. The cameras are looking at you; the people are there howling for your blood. A guy is punching me to pieces. It's all very basic.

> Chris Eubank, world super-middleweight
> champion whose fight with Michael Watson
> left Watson semi-paralysed and still in
> hospital at the time of writing.

Many people, however, if they are honest, have an

ambivalent attitude towards boxing. While deep down we question whether such a barbarous sport has a place in our society, we also enjoy watching it. Frank Bruno and Henry Cooper, former British heavyweight champions, are among the most popular men in Britain.

Professional boxing has been banned in some countries in Europe, for example, Norway, Sweden and Iceland. The British Medical Association has called for the banning of the sport in Britain while at the same time Dr Adrian Whiteson, the British Boxing Board of Control's chief medical officer, seeks to ensure that the sport is as safe as possible in the circumstances.

> We make no excuses that boxing is a dangerous sport, but then so are many other sports. Boxers know the risks that they take when they enter the ring.

Boxing has traditionally had a place in public schools, and recently the chairman of the Sports Council, Peter Yarranton, has said:

> Boxing is a super sport which gives youngsters in particular tremendous confidence in the art of self-defence.

On the other hand Dr David Bosher, director of the Pain Research Institute, was quoted in *The Times* last year:

Throwing Christians to the lions in ancient Rome was so much better. At least only one contestant suffered. In boxing both participants pay the price.

A few years ago the Churches Council for Health and Healing published an occasional paper "Boxing: a Christian Comment". The paper summarized the purpose of the human body as:

1. The temple of the Holy Spirit (1 Corinthians 6:10).

2. The body is further dignified by its use as a model for the body of Christ.

3. It referred to the doctrine of the incarnation in which God "honours human flesh and life".

4. The essential message of the Gospel is the creation of health or wholeness or salvation.

The report found it impossible to reconcile a sport which sought to inflict deliberate damage to the temple of the Holy Spirit with Christian principles.
The report concluded:

It is, then, for both medical and Christian reasons, that the working party feels bound to discourage rather than encourage boxing.

On the other hand, there are many boxers, trainers and managers who are Christians and who feel that boxing is part of their Christian life and a legitimate area in which to serve God. George Foreman, a former heavyweight champion of the world who made a comeback to fight for the world title at the age of 42, and who is also minister of a church, is one outstanding example.

WBA world lightweight champion Ray Mancini defended his title against Duk Koo Kim. Mancini knocked out his opponent who later died from the injuries sustained. Afterwards Mancini said, "I just hope people will understand that in this profession it's one of the risks we take. I didn't intend to hurt him." The question is can any boxer honestly say, "I didn't intend to hurt him"? While one can accept that he wished Kim no serious injury the fact is that the intention of boxing is to hurt one's opponent.

Drugs

Drug-taking is a particular form of cheating. The problem of drugs in sport is much older than many of us realize. There have been reports of drug misuse since 1865. However, drugs effectively made their appearance as a serious issue in the locker rooms in the fifties. Now when an athlete runs faster, jumps further, or throws further than before there is an immediate suspicion that the performance is not natural but drug-enhanced.

The issue put simply is that drugs and other substances are being taken not to cure an illness but to enhance performance. The main categories of banned substances are:

1. Stimulants
2. Narcotic analgesics
3. Anabolic steroids
4. Beta blockers
5. Diuretics

The various drugs have differing purposes. Steroids, for example, allow athletes to train longer and harder with a faster recovery period thereby allowing another training session quicker. Beta blockers, on the other hand, lower the heart rate and so steady the hand, a help in skilled sports.

Drug testing is now widely in force to counteract drug abuse. Athletes, for example, are tested on a random selection basis at competitions and also at any time during the year. In 1991 accredited laboratories carried out 84,088 drug tests worldwide. Part of the preparation for the 1992 Olympics included a huge new laboratory to cope with demand during the games.

As Eastern Europe has opened up in the last few years many people's suspicions that there has been a state-regulated drugs system in place for several years have been confirmed.

A disturbing aspect of the whole subject is the increasing evidence of the ploys used by athletes to avoid detection, including introducing "clean" urine into the bladder just prior to the test. Another sinister aspect is that new drugs are being developed which are impossible to detect.

On the other hand there is the fear of an innocent athlete being found guilty. This could happen through a laboratory accident or by a deliberate mislabelling/ switching of samples. Kriss Akabusi admits that it is a real concern.

> I always have the fear that someone is going to slip me something, somebody will be really mean and put something in my drinking bottle. I know that if I tested positive no one would believe me.

The most notorious case of drug abuse was probably Ben Johnson who came first in the 100 metres at the 1988 Olympics, only to test positive and be disqualified. The question immediately raised was how many of his previous records and wins should also now be discounted.

Johnson's coach, Charlie Francis, later said that he had been astounded that Ben had tested positive – not because he thought Johnson was innocent but because he thought they had been too clever. He was astonished as Ben's main drug had been an injectable form of steroid, furazabol, and "I knew it couldn't be detected since the IOC's lab equipment had not been programmed to identify it". He added that he did not believe that Johnson had cheated. "Cheating is doing something nobody else is doing." In 1992 Johnson again tested positive and was banned for life.

In the run-up to the 1992 Olympics Katrin Krabbe, double world champion sprinter, failed a test, received a four-year ban, appealed and was cleared and then had the ban reinstated and later reduced to one year. Butch Reynolds, the American 400 metres runner, protested his innocence of a drug offence and ban vociferously, to the point of appealing to the US Supreme Court which ruled that he must be allowed to take part in the American Olympic trials even though IAAF had ruled that he would not be allowed to take part in the Games under any circumstances. Incidents like these, whatever the outcome, inevitably tarnish the image of the sport.

At the 1992 Olympics British sprinter Jason Livingstone and weightlifters Andrew Saxton and Andrew Davies were sent home after results of drugs tests prior to the Olympics proved positive. The case of the two weightlifters illustrated the complexity of the drugs issue. The drug which they used was Clenbuterol and in the ensuing weeks there was a major debate among sports administrators as to whether or not Clenbuterol was a banned drug. At the time of writing the ban has been lifted. However, the case is likely to go to appeal.

The temptation to use drugs is very real. Jonah Barrington, six-time winner of the British Open squash title, quoted by Hemery, said that he never seriously considered taking drugs as a player "because I would know I had cheated". However he finds the dilemma greater as a coach.

It would be difficult for me as a coach to know whether I would continue with someone whom I felt had the ability to get to very near the top, but wasn't actually going to make it unless they took drugs.

Even Mr Clean himself, Kriss Akabusi, admits that he considered drugs when in 1986 he was at the crossroads in his career, feeling that he lacked the basic speed to remain competitive at world class in the 400 metres flat.

He reasoned, "Maybe I have reached my full potential . . . maybe the only way forward is to take drugs". In the end he decided against it because of the consequences of being caught:

I was already an established international athlete. If I was caught taking drugs all my achievements to date would be assumed to be drug-assisted. I was in the army and if I had been caught taking drugs not only would my athletics career have gone down the pan but my military career as well.

Roger Black, writing in *The Times* shortly before the 1992 Olympics, commented on the issue:

I used to feel frustrated by public comment on this subject. Now I feel sadness as well because the sport is suffering from a problem that, if not dealt with properly, will result in the next generation believing that the only way to achieve athletic success is by artificial means. I often wonder what goes on in the mind of a cheating athlete; morality obviously plays no part in his or her thought process and sporting ethics can be ruled out altogether.

The taking of banned drugs is a form of cheating. However, it is cheating only because the substance in question comes within the list of banned drugs within a particular sport. Every top athlete takes whatever special food and supplements suit their particular event and its training requirements in an attempt to gain an edge over an opponent. As Kriss Akabusi says, if he discovered that eating asparagus half an hour before a race helped his performance, he would do it but he wouldn't tell anyone!

One is reminded me of the story about Geoff Boycott and Basil D'Oliveira on the England tour of Australia where all the England team were having trouble reading Johnny Gleason when batting with D'Oliveira. D'Oliveira came down to Boycott and said, "I've worked out how to read him." Boycott replied, "So have I but don't tell all the others." It's quite an amusing story of selfishness overruling team spirit. Although it has no bearing on drug-taking and is denied by Boycott.

Conclusion

David Hemery in his conclusion to the chapter on
Gamesmanship quotes an opinion: "If you can't win
fairly, you don't deserve to win", and goes on to say
that once the rules of a sport have been broken, the
game has been changed. This must be the ideal.

However, it may not be very realistic to expect it
to be universally adopted in professional sport. There
the stakes are so high that people will continue to
seek to extract a victory by any means at all. There
is also the question of whether it is legitimate to break
the rules and accept the consequences, as discussed
above in relation to the professional foul.

It cannot be denied however that the examples of
good sportsmanship quoted in the chapter shine out
like a beacon. That is sport as it is intended with a
recognition that the game is in fact bigger than one
particular match and who wins it.

The Christian attitude to all this is probably best
encapsulated in the words of Jesus in the Sermon on
the Mount. "In everything, do to others what you
would have them do to you" (Matthew 7:12). Unless
we would be happy for an opponent to use a particular
play against us, we should not use it ourselves.

The life of the Christian is also to show the fruit
of the Spirit, "love, joy, peace, patience, kindness,
goodness, faithfulness, gentleness and self-control"
(Galatians 5:22, 23). That is a monumental challenge

to us as we play our sport.

Playing sport in this attitude is unlikely to lead to any conflict with the laws. However, working it all out in practice in every situation will not be easy.

CHAPTER FOUR

And They Pay You To Do It?

Those of us who have routine – even boring – jobs find it hard to understand the pressure of the life style of the professional sportsperson. "Fancy being paid to do what you love", we think. Moreover the sporting superstars earn more in a week, perhaps, than we make in a year. We watch Steve Davis coolly collect another £100,000 in prize money and think maybe we could do the same.

The pressures in the world of professional sport are however intense. George Best and Bjorn Borg are just two of sports superstars who opted out when right at the top. They had enough of the pressures. Arguably the greatest football talent the country has ever seen, Best helped Manchester United to the League championship in 1967 and the European Cup – the first ever win by an English club – the following year. However by the age of 27 he had given it all up.

Best claims that it was disenchantment with football which led to his departure.

It had nothing to do with women and booze, car

crashes and court cases. It was purely and simply
football. A great team went into decline. United
made no real attempt to buy the best replacements
available. I was left struggling among fellas who
should not have been allowed through the door at
Old Trafford.

While there is no doubt truth in that, the *Observer*'s
football writer, Hugh McIlvanney, suggests:

Had his life and his personality not been in such
confusion, he might have withstood those miseries
on the field.

The biggest pressure is perhaps the pressure to succeed. In sport it is said "You are only as good as
your last game". Reputations count for nothing. If you
cannot "do the business" today, you are not wanted
any more.

No job can be more precarious than that of the
football manager. Success yesterday is irrelevant
today. Terry Neill describes the moment poignantly
in his book *Revelations of a Football Manager*:

The telephone call confirmed everything. All the
feelings and instincts developed over 25 years in
the game told me this was my moment of truth. It
was a routine call from Ken Friar, Arsenal's manag-
ing director, to discuss the day's business.

Halfway through our conversation Ken suddenly
said: "Oh by the way, the chairman wants to see
you at 9 a.m. tomorrow." . . . After 18 years with

Arsenal Football Club as a player and manager all my loyalty and affection for the club meant nothing. Business was business. I was about to be sacked! Thousands of managers have been sacked since the Football League was formed in 1888. They don't like it but they have to accept it, because not all of them can be winners.

In some sports there is the constant travelling. Top golfers and tennis players compete about forty weeks of the year. This adds up to a gruelling schedule of travel. Either the family travel with you or you rarely see them. Bernhard Langer describes it as "the hardest part of the job. Living in hotel rooms – even the best hotels with all the luxury that they can provide – is no comparison with home." Golfers who travel the world are used to having a courtesy car to meet them. However as Bernhard says, it is not so much a courtesy car as a courtesy truck that he needs for his family and all their stuff!

The problem is arguably worse for the sportswoman. In many ways the problems facing a woman in professional sport are not unlike those facing any career-minded woman. To be successful involves a high level of commitment, absence from home, possibly travel overseas: am I prepared to pay the price? While it is true that men are faced with the same issues, they tend to be more starkly presented to women, because of society's expectations of women.

Maintaining a steady relationship while working in

professional sport is not easy. In golf, for example, a player's husband has to decide whether to be part of the golf tour or not. If not, he must accept the separation from his wife for up to half the year. If he travels with her, in what capacity will it be? Some husbands caddy for their wives. However, things said in the heat of a pressured moment can damage the ongoing relationship. Either way it is not easy.

The social implications of professional sport are immense. If you are constantly on the move playing tennis or golf around the world, it is difficult to develop a normal social life. You are not at home enough or in a predictable enough pattern to develop a normal social life. As a result the golf/tennis/squash tour becomes a world in its own right, a self-contained compartment within society.

Incidentally one implication of this is the difficulty experienced in giving up. There are many professional sportspeople – both men and women – who are not good enough and not really making a living – but who cannot face the prospect of giving it up. They know no other world.

For the sportsperson there is the constant need to maintain your form and your self-confidence. A leading professional golfer who has been highly successful for the last few years told me that she always starts the new season wondering if she will be as good as she was the previous year. She never feels that she can take anything for granted.

How often do we watch a top sportsperson on TV

and say, "I wish I could play like that". We are justified in envying the natural ability of the champion,
but do we also envy the work put in to reach that
level? Would you like to play tennis like Steffi Graf?
OK, start practising six or eight hours a day!

Someone once called Gary Player lucky. He
replied, "Yes, I am lucky. The funny thing is, the
more I practise, the luckier I get!"

Insecurity

There is in professional sport an insecurity that is
found in few walks of life. Guy McIntyre, an offensive
guard with the San Francisco 49ers, once said, "I
realize that I'm just in the team until they find someone, bigger, stronger or that they can pay less to." It
is to his credit that he was able to view his status with
such realism. It is said that the initials of the NFL,
the National Football League, also stand for "Not for
Long", a timely reminder of the shortness of the
career at the top level in American football.

Shirl Hoffman has expressed the cynicism of professional sport as

> bodies as instruments of destruction, expendable
> machinery designed and developed to test the
> limits of expendability of the bodies of those with
> whom they compete.[1]

Because success is everything, there is no room for sentiment. There is a great deal of cruelty in professional sport. Football club managers are sacked, players are not given new contracts. It is a tough world. Your best mate is after your job! Players are ordinary people, they feel hurt just as much as anyone else.

Graham Daniels, now the Christians in Sport evangelist, was playing for Cambridge United. His contract was up at the end of the season. He was waiting anxiously to know if he would get another contract or if he should start looking for another job. After the game on the Saturday, the manager said, "Well played. Another game like that on Tuesday and I'll be offering you a new contract." "Great," thought Graham. "If I can only do all right on Tuesday, my future is secure." On the Monday, Graham read in the paper that the manager had been sacked. The new manager did not renew the contracts of any of the existing players. Graham's career in professional football came to an abrupt end!

The pressure on the England football manager is perhaps greater than on most people in the world of sport. The nation wants the team to be successful. If it isn't the manager has to carry the can. In the run up to the 1990 World Cup, the tabloid press launched a vicious attack on manager Bobby Robson, urging him to resign.

After one disappointing result the tabloid headlines were "In God's name go". England's next game was against a North African country. The after-match headlines were "For the sake of Allah, go"! His successor Graham Taylor is often depicted as a turnip-head in the same papers.

Incidentally England managers may like to note that Zulu football teams have a witch doctor, called the Inyanga, in addition to the coach and manager. His duties include sacrificing a goat pre-season and administering magic potions on the day of the game. The good news is that when the team loses it is the Inyanga and not the manager who is sacked.

An amusing – though less so at the time – example of the pressure of life in professional sport involves Alan West. When Alan was playing for Millwall, the author once found himself standing with Alan outside the Millwall ground about an hour before kick-off. Alan had been dropped.

A well-known and larger-than-life Millwall supporter came over to Alan and said, "Are you playing today?" Alan replied politely, "No, I've been dropped." "Great!" exclaimed the supporter, "That's the best news I've heard all day!" and went rushing off to tell his mates. With fans like that who needs enemies?

Family life

Professional sport impinges on family life to a great extent. For one thing you do not get many weekends off. There is also the problem of trying to live a normal life. It is a common problem for a footballer's wife to go out with her husband, even to church, and find him the centre of attention and herself totally ignored. Everyone wants to meet him, to bask in the reflected glory, but nobody is interested in her.

Before she met her future husband Alan, Jill Comfort hardly knew that football existed. It is interesting to see how she, initially an outsider, perceived the world of professional football in which Alan worked.

One of the first things I had to learn was the pressure involved in professional football. I don't think that anyone who isn't involved can have any idea of what the pressures are. Increasingly I have become part of it. Before a game Alan needed quiet to build himself up and I just had to keep out of the way of that process. When he has a bad game everyone is part of the process. It is like a morgue. Sometimes when I hear that they have lost, I dread the evening and the following week. I don't mean that Alan was difficult to live with, he wasn't. It is just that when the team loses there is a sense of deflation. You have to live with the fact that you lost until your next match.

Footballers take a lot of criticism – from the manager, the coach, the crowd etc. That can linger in their minds to the next game. It has to be worked through.

Another thing which I sometimes found difficult to cope with is the unpredictability of the life style.

Where are you going to be in a year's time? Where will you be in three years? My own career is more predictable. I can stay until I decide it is time to leave. I have much more control over my job than Alan has over his.

When Jill and Alan got married football again made its presence felt. Alan was playing for Leyton Orient at the time. They set the date of their wedding, having carefully checked the football fixtures. The wedding day was to be a week after the last possible day of the season, including play-offs. However the dates of the play-offs were put back a week. (At the end of the season the top three clubs in the fourth division are promoted to the third division wih the clubs finishing fourth, fifth, sixth and seventh playing off for the fourth promotion place.)

That was a potential problem but a fairly remote one. For most of the season there seemed little chance that Orient would reach them. Then, with a late run, Orient moved up the table and secured a play-off place. Even then they had to win their first match before a clash between the wedding and the play-off final became a reality.

Orient made the final. The wedding was set for 3 p.m. in Bangor, Northern Ireland. Orient were to play Wrexham in the play-off final at the same time in London. Alan had a problem!

The time of the wedding was put back until 5 p.m. Orient brought the kick-off forward to 12 noon, ostensibly to avoid a clash with an England international match which was on live television. In reality it was to have Alan's services.

Alan played for Orient at 12.00. The kick-off was delayed as the crowd was larger than expected. In the end Orient won 2–1. Alan went by Sunday Express helicopter – provided in exchange for the exclusive story – to Heathrow where British Midland had agreed to hold the flight. At Belfast International Airport, he transferred to a private plane to Newtownards Airport. A police escort got him to the church on time.

Now that he is no longer playing professional football, Alan sees more clearly how obsessive professional sport is:

> Our whole week was geared to football. If Jill and I were invited out on a Thursday or Friday evening, either I would say "I can't go. It's too close to Saturday's game" or I would go and insist on being home by ten. Everyone and everything had to fit around me and my football. Now we can decide together to go out or not.

Gayle Nelson has travelled with husband Larry as much as possible during the last fifteen years that he has played tournament golf. Lately as their children have got older, Gayle has been able to travel less:

> It's been a big adjustment because I enjoyed being with him a lot and being on tour. It was hard to

continue when the boys became school age. It was like having my feet in two pairs of shoes and neither was as comfortable as I would have liked.

For the sportsman travelling without his family, there are particular pressures to be encountered. Christian tennis player, Ken Flach, spoke of this on a BBC radio interview:

It is a life of great temptation. There are many female admirers around the court. When you are travelling on your own you have a lot of time on your hands. With God's help and because of my desire to please Him, I am able to resist the temptations. The biggest help is reading the Bible to gain the strength that I need.

Strange though it may seem there is a type of girl who hangs around sportspeople with the clear intention of going to bed with a star for the kudos that is supposed to be found in the achievement. Ken Flach is far from alone in finding this a difficult situation to deal with.

Christmas

For most people Christmas is a time of rest and relaxation. For many it is a week of work, eating and drinking too much. For many sportspeople, however, the Christmas period is just another day at the office.

There is a full programme of football league fixtures on Boxing Day so professional footballers have to be careful what they eat. Many footballers will spend part of their Christmas Day travelling to the next day's match and will spend Christmas night in a hotel.

Joanne Starbuck is in her second generation of football-dominated Christmases. The daughter of a footballer, she then married one. Grin and bear it is Joanne's attitude.

> I've always had good Christmases, but it always had to fit around football. When Philip (her husband, now Huddersfield Town) was at Nottingham Forest they always trained on Christmas morning, were allowed home for a quick lunch and to open presents, then they always went to a hotel for Christmas night in preparation for the Boxing Day match. Our real Christmas celebration tended to be on Boxing night.

When Glenn Hoddle left Tottenham to play for Monaco in the French league, the six-week break in the French football season in December and January gave him the first opportunity to spend a normal Christmas with his family.

Professional cricketers often spend Christmas on tour. Vic Marks, former England Test cricketer and now cricket correspondent of the *Observer*, has spent three Christmases on tour with England. He describes Christmas on tour as "enforced merriment".

The Christmas Day programme on tour might consist of a midnight service, some kind of turkey dinner and the team taking it in turn to entertain each other.

In a sense Christmas on tour resembles an obstacle course, something to survive with the minimum of discomfort. We feel obliged to enjoy ourselves and yet we would all prefer to be shivering in our own homes.

Money

Perhaps the biggest change in the world of sport over the last twenty years is the sums of money involved. A recent survey listed one or two sportspeople with an annual income in excess of £10 million and several over £1 million.

In a previous chapter we looked at some outstanding examples of sportsmanship from the past and wondered whether they could still happen in the context of today's greater commercial pressures.

Like it or not sport is now a £-multi-million industry. If thousands of spectators are paying millions to watch, then surely it is reasonable for the players to get a piece of the action. While the thought of all sport being amateur, for the love of participation and so on, is a nice thought, it is not a realistic one.

The progress in achievements in the breaking of records has come because competitors are now fitter and better trained because it is their job not their hobby. One cannot have this level of dedication and the consequent higher achievement without adequate reward.

If the love of money is the root of all evil, and it is easier for a camel to go through the eye of a needle, how do Christians survive in this commercial jungle of professional sport? Few people are better qualified to comment on the subject than Bernhard Langer whose prize money in 1991 exceeded two million dollars to say nothing of sponsorship, endorsements, appearance money, etc.

In an interview in *Women and Golf* in 1992 he said:

> If the professional tournament market is prepared to offer us $1 million to play each week, that's not my fault. In fact I see absolutely nothing wrong with it. It means I can earn more money to give to people who need it.

Langer's answer seems the correct one. As a Christian there is no reason why he should not use his God-given talents to the full. Like everyone else he is accountable to God for his stewardship of his money.

It can also be said that for every one person in professional sport earning millions, there are thousands who struggle to make ends meet. I think too that the man in the street probably feels less resentful of the earnings of the sportsperson whose talents are there for all to see than of, say, the British Insurance

Company chairman whose chief executive was paid £6 million in 1992.

Life in the public eye

When a magazine asked Kriss Akabusi what his secret phobia was he shocked a lot of people by saying "people". One might have thought that the extrovert Akabusi would have said the opposite. However, as he elaborated on the phobia, he explained that the fear of people arises from a feeling of always being on show.

Kriss Akabusi is unable to walk round the supermarket without being recognized, asked for his autograph, etc. Most of the time it's fine, but sometimes it's a hassle. In any case all sportspeople know what is worse than being asked for your autograph – not being asked!

Sportspeople in the public eye get fan mail, offers of marriage, etc. They are constantly being asked to support this or that good cause, to donate as appropriate a signed match shirt or international vest to be auctioned for charity. Kriss Akabusi receives easily a hundred of these per year. The trouble is that everyone thinks that they are the only one who has written and are therefore disappointed if it is not possible for them to receive the latest Great Britain vest signed by the entire Olympic squad.

As more independent learning methods are intro-

duced in schools, young people are constantly looking
for topics on which to do a project. When in doubt,
do it on Kriss Akabusi. Kriss receives questionnaires
– what do you eat before races, how often do you
train, which opponent to you fear? One food science
project wanted him to make a note of everything that
he ate and drank for a week. Most of these seem to
come in the build-up to the world championships,
Olympic games, etc. Kriss assists with as many of
these as he can within the limited time available.

Being a Christian athlete brings its own pressure.
The few high-profile Christian sportspeople in the
UK receive a multitude of invitations to speak at
churches. It is an interesting assumption that because
one can run fast or score spectacular goals, one must
also be an authority on the Christian faith and an
accomplished after-dinner speaker. In truth most
Christian sportspeople are neither.

It is often sad how little understanding churches
show of the pressures on Christian sportspeople.
Churches expect the sportsperson to travel hundreds
of miles to take part in a church service. Often if the
invitation is declined the response is something like
"Oh dear, we would have thought that you were in
favour of evangelism."

Thus the Christian sportsperson is made to feel
guilty as well. And the church which ought to be
rejoicing that there is a Christian at the top level in
sport and praying for that person, is rather adding to
the pressure on him.

Lisa Opie is very aware of being watched by fellow squash players:

> The more difficult area in which to be a Christian is being watched. If I slip up and swear on court or even if I'm just having a drink, someone will say "I'm surprised at you and you a Christian too". It's OK for them to swear all day but if I slip up once, they jump on me. Another area is the temptation to follow the crowd. At times, especially when I'm travelling on the tour, you have to be very disciplined and go off on your own – to make time to read the Bible, go to church or whatever.

Ups and downs

It is in the nature of sport that there are constant ups and downs. The Wimbledon champion can lose in the first round next week. To succeed in professional sport one needs to learn at an early stage, with Kipling, to "meet with triumph and disaster and treat those two imposters just the same".

A year is a long time in the life of a professional footballer. The period from Easter 1991 to Easter 1992 saw Dennis Bailey experience successively the highs and lows that the game can bring.

Towards the end of the 1991 season Dennis was a Birmingham City player. However, he was out of favour, not on the team. Gerry Francis, who was

manager of Bristol Rovers, signed Dennis on loan.
He did well for Bristol Rovers.

At the end of the season Gerry Francis moved from
Bristol Rovers to become manager of First Division
Queen's Park Rangers. One of the first things that he
did was to make an offer to Birmingham City for
Dennis Bailey. Dennis jumped at the chance to join
a First Division club.

Dennis had a reasonable start to the season, played,
scored, lost his place, regained it. Then on 1 January
1992, Queen's Park Rangers played Manchester
United in a match shown live on television. QPR
pulled off the shock of the season, beating Manchester
United 4–1, with Dennis scoring three goals. From
an obscure Third Division reserve, he had become a
successful First Division player. He was pictured in
all the papers the following day with most of the
papers commenting on his Christian faith. The *Daily
Mirror*'s main back page headline was: "Praise the
Lord".

A month later Dennis sustained a groin injury from
which recovery was slow. The team had a successful
time when he was out and he ended the season unable
to regain his place.

How does a Christian player react to all this?
Dennis has no doubt that his Christian faith makes a
difference.

It helps me keep life in perspective and to see that
life is not just about yourself but about other people

too. Knowing God and His purposes helps me view life from a different perspective. I could definitely say that Jesus has been my rock in all the ups and downs. Sometimes you think the downs are never going to end but God has always put it together in the end. He never said it would be easy but He's always been there.

Justyn Cassell plays rugby for Saracens. In 1992 he was sent off after an incident with a Bath player, Andy Robinson. In his view he was an entirely innocent victim of the situation. Yet the next day his sending-off made the headlines on the sports pages.

The irony was that things could hardly have been going better for Justyn. It was the last league game of the season against Bath. He felt that Saracens could give Bath, the champions-elect, a run for their money. Afterwards, he and his wife were going out with some of the other players and their wives. A month or so later he was off to New Zealand with the England "B" squad.

Now to the incident itself. After the ball had gone, Andy Robinson held on to Justyn's legs, he struggled to free himself and accidentally caught Robinson in the face with his boot. The touch-judge flagged, drew the referee's attention to the incident and Justyn was sent off.

As a committed Christian, Justyn sought to deal with the experience within the context of his Christian faith.

My initial thought was: "I didn't do it. Why should I be sent off?" I just couldn't believe it. As I walked off thoughts flashed through my mind, that I would miss the England "B" tour and so on. There was a feeling of disbelief that it was actually happening. As I sat in the changing room I was asking, "Why did it happen, is it satanic, is it of God or what?" I wondered was it God's way of saying that I wasn't to go on the "B" tour. After the game lots of people made encouraging comments to me which helped.

In fact the first person who spoke to Justyn when he reached the changing room that day was his wife, Melissa. She fought her way through the crowds and stewards to comfort him.

The Sunday papers painted a very black picture of the incident and I was frustrated, thinking that's not what happened. But the Monday papers supported me.

After the game I prayed, "Lord, I believe that you are in this. I accept what has happened. Whatever you want to come out of this is fine by me." He gave me a peace about it. I knew in my heart that I hadn't done it and I knew that something positive would come out of it. So I was at peace. I believe there was a reason for why it happened even though I don't know what the reason was.

The disciplinary hearing was something of a fudge. They accepted that Justyn's use of the boot had not been "wilful" but said it had been "careless" and gave him a two-week suspension. Had he received the normal 60-day suspension, he would have missed the England "B" tour.

This is a fine example of a Christian playing his sport with a Christian motivation, accepting adversity and giving the whole situation to God.

Growing in the Christian life

At an open forum meeting on the Men's professional golf tour, one golfer asked. "How can one grow as a Christian if one never gets to church on a Sunday because of Sunday play?" It was a good question.

Sandy Mayer who was one of the world's top tennis players in the early 80s commented on the issue:

> Ten years ago I would have said it was questionable whether a Christian joining the tennis circuit could have prospered spiritually and grown in his faith. Based on what has happened in the last two years, I would say that there is light on the tennis court, and that there is an opportunity for someone to incorporate Christian living and tennis.

> *The Times*, December 31 1985

While he did not say so explicitly, there is no doubt that he was referring to the tennis ministry of Fritz Glaus who has travelled on the tour for several years.

The support of fellow-Christians in the sport is also

a help. Corey Pavin, the leading money winner on the US golf tour in 1991 attributes his coming to faith and growth as a Christian to the fellowship on the tour.

I know that without the Bible study and fellowship on tour I may not have come to be a Christian this soon. The ability to go to someone on the tour to discuss anything you want to, especially the Bible, is very important. The fellowship that we all have here is critical, and knowing that we are going to get good sound Christian advice is something we all feel strongly about.

I recently told a tour pro how good I felt about the fact that because of Christ I have something very strong in common with anyone who comes to the Bible study, even though we may not know them from any past experience on tour. I feel immediately like they're my friend. This is a very strong thing and a very powerful bond.

The world of professional sport is without doubt an exciting one with great rewards for those who reach the top. It is also a world where the pressure to achieve is great, with everything depending on your ability to "do the business". As the saying in sport goes "You are only as good as your last game". This breeds great insecurity.

CHAPTER FIVE

Crisis Points

Sportspeople are not heroes, they are humans. They live a very intense life style with many ups and downs. They live under immense pressure all the time. They have the pressure from the crowd, big pressure from the press – because they write what they want. Sportspeople have to be very careful of what they say to anyone. Pressure from the team – there is always somebody after your job.

Sponsors invest a lot of work and money in the sport and they want the sportsperson to win – because the sponsor wants to make money. Because of the increase of sponsorship we now have a different athlete.

Fear follows every athlete. Fear of losing. The more important the meeting the bigger the fear, fear of losing your place, meeting someone better. Fear of injury, hurt at the wrong time, fear and anxiety are enormous.

They have family problems because in many sports they are on tour all the time. The sportsperson is very protected from fans – so there is a lot of loneliness because the barriers work both ways. They can be bored and when they are bored they go into drugs and drinking. They are so insecure and superstitious.

Ordinary men and women, whose sole distinction is their ability to kick or handle a ball or run very fast, become the superstars of an entire nation, the role models for millions. Companies pay them to wear and endorse their products. Media attention invades their privacy; their families, their habits, their diet, their financial situations all become public property. They are lifted high on a pedestal of fame and relative fortune; but in Britain certainly the media delights in a fallen hero. The pressure on these often young and impressionable people is enormous.

In many ways the pressures which confront the sportsperson are the same as those faced in business. There is, however, one major difference. In sport, gifted athletes reach the top in their chosen tree much quicker than in corporate society. The world's top tennis players are often teenagers. Ryan Giggs has been around for so long that people are amazed to realize that the birthday the Manchester United star celebrated at the end of 1992 was only his nineteenth.

What is more the life span of a athlete is short. An electrician can be an electrician for life. In sport if you have 10–15 years at the top, you can count yourself fortunate.

Loss of form

One of the great fears of the sportsperson is loss of form. Your reputation is built on your ability to perform at a certain level in your sport. However in a world where "you are only as good as your last game", the fear of losing your form and confidence is always in the background.

In the late 1970s Sue Barker was one of the world's top tennis players. She won the French Championship. She was a semi-finalist at Wimbledon. At her peak she was ranked fourth in the world. Then suddenly the wheels came off. She seemed to lose all confidence and her ranking dropped – out of the top ten, then twenty. Within five years she was 62nd. Why? There was a dog bite on the face which kept her off court for several months, a well publicized romance . . . but can anyone really explain what happened? Sue played tennis for a few more years but it never happened for her again at the really top level.

In the 1991 World Championship Steve Backley was favourite to win gold in the javelin. He did not even make the final. He had a bad day. He could not produce anything like his best form. Afterwards he was quoted: "They say javelin is all about rhythm. I couldn't even hear the music!" However, Backley bounced back to win an Olympic bronze medal.

Few people have suffered losses of form as dramatically as the German golfer, Bernhard Langer.

Bernhard was at the height of his career when he was afflicted by the yips, an inability to control one's putter or the ball on short putts which the player would normally expect to hole without any problem. It is a churning of the stomach, a condition of extreme nervousness which can either prevent a player from moving the putter or force him to jerk it.

In his book *When The Iron Is Hot*, Bernhard describes it clearly.

> I began to lose control of my putter as soon as I got close to the hole. . . People were coming out to watch me but in the manner of those people who go to car races hoping to see a crash. . . I rarely let them down. To the spectators it must have been like watching a man suffer a very public nervous breakdown as I stood over my ball, muscles tensing, colour draining from my face.

The yips have afflicted Bernhard three times during his career but each time he has come back. Each period of several months was a nightmare with confidence at such a low level that even picking up a golf club was a nightmare. During this period he received advice from every quarter – try hypnosis, get a new putter, hold the putter more loosely, hold the putter tighter, change your grip and so on.

His reaction to the problem was typical. He worked harder than ever. He spent hour after hour on the practice putting green. He also developed his own techniques for dealing with the problem. When the problem appeared for the second time (in 1982) he started putting with the left hand below the right. The approach was so successful that in 1984, the statistics show him as the best putter in Europe!

Four years later the problems resurfaced and he adopted another new technique, gripping the left arm with the right arm trapping the shaft of the putter against the left forearm. Ironically in 1990 he was again top of the putting statistics.

Looking back on the bad times Bernhard acknowledges that at times it was only the support of his family and his faith in the Lord that kept him going. He confesses that the experience took him to the brink:

> There were many times when I prayed about it and said, "If it is your will, God, that I should continue to be a golfer help me out of this mystery. Give me some idea of what I should be doing, what I should be changing, but if you don't want me to be a golfer whatever your will is just let me know so that I can change my life and go the direction you want me to be.

When a player suffers a loss of form coaches are constantly looking for a reason. A player's beliefs can get the blame. This is often expressed as "You've lost your competitive edge . . . you don't get angry. I want to hear you swearing at the opposition."

Alan Comfort had an amusing example when he

was playing for Leyton Orient. He wasn't playing very well and the manager called him in to ask about it. Alan told him that he was feeling a bit under pressure in his private life which might be affecting his form. The manager looked relieved and said that he had been worried that Alan's Christian faith was the problem. If it was just a domestic pressure then there was nothing to worry about!

Disappointment

Jonathan Edwards approached the 1992 Olympics in which he would represent Britain in the Triple Jump with real hope and anticipation. He had a genuine chance of a medal. The anticipation of the Olympics was all the greater because at one stage he had not expected to be there. Jonathan had decided that he would not compete if the triple jump was on a Sunday. When he read in the Olympic schedule that the event qualifying stage was on a Saturday, he feared the worst. However, Sunday was a rest day with the final on the Monday. Jonathan gave thanks to God.

On Saturday 1 August Jonathan failed to find his true form. Three bad jumps and he was out of the competition. This is his own account of the 1992 Olympics:

Any athlete will tell you that the run-ups to major

games are fraught, with little niggling injuries and
nagging doubts, yet as I recall my lead-in to Barcelona my only thought is that I couldn't have wished
for better. Physically I was in excellent shape and
spiritually I was aware of God's hand on me in a
very real way and felt strong confirmation that God
wanted me to be an athlete. I honestly felt that it
was God's will for me to succeed whatever that
entailed.

As Linford Christie fulfilled his Olympic dream,
mine came to an unheralded end. I don't think I
have ever felt such pain and anguish. It had to be
a bad dream; I would wake up any minute and do
it for real – anything to give relief from the reality.
Could I have heard God so wrongly? Could I carry
on as an athlete? I was frightened too – my whole
future and my wife Alison's also seemed blown
apart in just three awful jumps.

One encouraging aspect was that the season was
far from over and I still had many opportunities to
show what might have happened in Barcelona. In
reality over the next weeks as I strove to regain
my form things only got worse. From jumping 17
metres plus consistently, 16 metres plus became a
real difficulty. This was harder than the Olympics
and now my confidence in my own ability was
shattered.

A lot of the time I was numb to it all, but sometimes the reality of what was happening would
break through and in those times the pain was

almost too much to bear. Within athletics I felt talentless, uninteresting, insignificant and often just wanted to run away during competitions because I couldn't bear the humiliation.

As a Christian from childhood, Jonathan constantly sought God in the traumas going on around him.

I realized that God had called me into athletics and nothing had changed. Suddenly though I really had to trust God and not my own ability.

During all this I never felt that God was far away. I didn't understand, but I knew that God was working out His ways for good. "Why are you downcast O my Soul? Put your hope in God for I will yet praise Him, my Saviour and my God." I was learning again that my hope was to be in God and not in happy circumstances, and that, come what may, he is worthy to be praised. And in my heart God gave me an assurance that things wouldn't always be like this and an expectancy that he could turn things around and put wings on my feet at any time and restore my jumping form.

Having said that, I was not entirely prepared for Havana, Cuba on 26th September 1992 when I finished first in the World Cup triple jump with 17.34 metres, my third best ever and ironically enough to have given me fourth place in the Olympics! I can only say that it was a miracle. People will read this and think me simplistic and naive to say such a thing, but I know it to be true. The God

we serve is indeed mighty and I will never forget
Havana or Barcelona or who it is who gives me my
strength.

Failure

Most competitors fail – in the sense that there can
only be one winner. Yet when failure comes it can be
devastating. David Williams was a golf tournament
professional playing the European tour. After several
years making a reasonable living – ranked 34th in
1990 – he had a bad year in 1992. He finished 133rd.
Only the top 125 keep their card, the right to play
the tour the following year.

Williams had to go to the tour school and finish in
the top 40 to regain his card. The competition lasts
six days. On the final day he was doing OK. He
missed a putt from less than two feet. He dropped
shots at the 14th and 15th. He dropped another at
the 18th. He took one shot too many to make the top
40.

Afterwards he told Andrew Farrell of *Golf Weekly*:

I've tried so many things in the last three months.
Gimmicks, tips, got advice off people – I've even
gone to a psychologist – but it has to come from
within. The hardest thing is to believe in yourself.
You should be strong enough to cope but after
week after week of doubting yourself it's not

easy. . . "If you can trust yourself when all men
doubt you . . . you'll be a man my son".   Kipling

In 1988, when the Seoul Olympics took place, Angela
Pendrick was twelve. Her ambition was to swim in
the 1992 Games in the 400 metres. She had the potential, the talent. Over the next four years Angela
worked to bring the dream to fruition, training 16
hours a week, swimming some 40,000 metres a week.
The final hurdle was the Olympic trials.

Angela swam a good race, finishing in 4 minutes
19.73 seconds. It was only when she looked to the
scoreboard to check her time that she discovered, to
her horror, that she had been pipped by Samantha
Foggo who finished in 4:19.59. In a race where only
the winner was guaranteed Olympic selection, Angela
came second and missed out on the Olympics by 0.14
of a second. All she wanted to do was be on her own;
to get away from everyone. Four years' work gone in
0.14 of a second.

Fear of injury

The fear of injury is something that all sportspeople
live with. It is an occupational hazard. You depend
on your physical body to earn your living, yet you are
always just one bad fall away from a premature end.

Motor sports are by definition hazardous. Champion rally driver Ari Vatanen knows that better than

most. He acknowledges the danger: "The inherent danger may not be the sole attraction but it adds a certain spice to life." He adds, tongue in cheek perhaps, "I could never imagine getting the same satisfaction from stamp collecting for example".

Driving in a rally in Argentina in 1985, Ari had a horrendous accident. "We were driving down a long straight at high speed when suddenly I felt like the end of the world. I have no recollection of the actual accident, although I never lost consciousness completely. My seat broke and I was thrown all over the car." Ari's injuries included a broken leg, flattened knee, eight broken ribs, punctured lung, fractured cervical vertebra, other vertebrae damaged. After eighteen months Ari was back in rallying.

Mikie Heaton-Ellis was a promising National Hunt jockey, who had already ridden eleven winners when he rode at Huntingdon. Mikie's horse fell and another horse landed on top of him. His back was broken. He spent ten months in hospital and never walked again. (The fascinating story of Mikie's determined battle to become a successful racehorse trainer is told in our earlier book *Winning is not Enough*.)

In 1981 Steve Coppell of Manchester United and England was at his peak. He already had 42 England caps. At 26 he had a bright future ahead of him. A tackle by Josef Toth in an England–Hungary international shattered his knee. Fourteen months and three operations later he had to accept that his career as a professional footballer was over.

Another who suffered a similar fate was Alan Comfort. In 1989 Alan was 25. He was in his first season with Middlesbrough. He had made a great start to the season, being voted player of the month in his second month at the club.

In his third month he was playing against Newcastle United. He was running for the ball and something in his knee snapped. There was damage to the ligaments and kneecap. It was a freak incident but his career in professional football was over. There was treatment, surgery, physiotherapy, visits to more specialists. There was no cure.

From the moment it happened Alan admits that he feared the worst.

> In this kind of situation there are basically two types of people. The first type says, "I'm going to get fit regardless". The other type is scared stiff. I was the second one for some reason. From the moment I got injured I thought I was finished, I was frightened to death that I was finished. so every time I got pain I got frightened – that's just the kind of person I am. But I think most players have niggling doubts, that they're not going to come back, or they won't be the same. You can't escape that because you rely on your body so much.

Losing your career, no longer being as good as you were, is an experience common to man. However, it strikes the injured sportsperson in a more sudden and dramatic way than most. The fall from grace can be instantaneous. From being a star, you are suddenly not even worth watching. That can be a difficult experience to cope with.

Alan Comfort sums it up:

> You go from being worth an awful lot to people to absolutely nothing. When you begin to realize that, your self-respect just falls apart. You are nothing. You're less than that. People don't treat you well at all.

As a Christian how did Alan cope with it? Did he have the added pressure of wondering why God had allowed it all to happen?

> Yes, I don't think you can escape that. Every day I was saying why has this happened? From a Christian point of view it was always helpful to think that God knew why it was happening and that God was still in control.
>
> Things happen that you wish didn't happen, but ultimately you still have to believe that God has a great plan and that plan will still go ahead. God's wider plan still continues and you're still moving in the right direction. But I still can't understand why it happened.

Working out the theology of it all is not easy. Does God cause an injury to happen? Or does it just happen and does God then make the best out of it? What is beyond question is that God most certainly knew it was going to happen. Humanity is fragile. Injuries happen. Just because you are a Christian, you don't have any insurance against it. But the great thing is that you know that God is in control so that there's got to be something else for you.

When his football career ended Alan Comfort felt the call of God to preach. He went to college to prepare for ordination for the Church of England ministry. Does that affect his view of the injury?

What makes me feel that God has more control than we anticipate, was the fact that my particular knee injury was quite unusual. If I'd just ruptured my cruciate ligaments they could have been mended, but the damage to my kneecap just wasn't the normal thing and they couldn't do anything. It was almost as if God had a plan for me to go into the ministry and there was only a certain injury that could have made sure that I wouldn't have spent three years trying to get fit.

End of career

A related fear to that of sustaining a serious injury is the anticipation of the end of your career. The problem is that for many professional sportspeople there is nothing else in the world that you can now do. In professional football, for example, the norm is to leave school at sixteen and start an apprenticeship. You sacrifice further education. The career is good while it lasts but what do you do when it is all over?

As many as possible stay in the game, after all what other world do you know? But the number of openings for coaches and managers is limited. Others open a sports shop, hoping to trade on the famous name – but in reality a knowledge of business is more important – others take over a pub.

The Professional Footballers' Association gives study grants and careers guidance to players as they approach the end of their playing careers. Their help is appreciated but for many it is not an easy transition from player to ex-player.

One solution is to become a vicar. The author knows of four professional footballers, in addition to Alan Comfort, who have ended up in the Christian ministry, to say nothing of the odd athlete or cricketing bishop!

Being there

In a world of pressure and uncertainty where injury can end a career at its peak without a moment's notice, the need for a caring, supportive pastoral ministry is beyond question.

It is for that reason that chaplaincy has become an accepted part of the sports scene. Players and coaches have seen the value of having someone to talk to, to provide care, help, a listening ear, to be a pastoral safety net.

The case for chaplaincy was put very eloquently by George Best a few years ago in the BBC radio programme, *A word with Williams.* Speaking about the loneliness of his early days at Manchester United, he said:

> I have been saying for years that there is a need for someone to look after young professionals but I do not know one club that has ever done anything about it. I am talking about someone not necessarily connected with the club. If you have a problem and it is a little bit personal you don't want to go and talk to a trainer or coach or a manager or even other players. You want someone who can advise you, someone away from the playing side, away from the club family itself. I think that is why so many players get into trouble – they have no-one to advise them, they have no-one to turn to when things go wrong.

The concept of chaplaincy is a familiar one within the Christian ministry. There are industrial chaplains, school chaplains, military padres and hospital chaplains for example. The idea of a sports chaplain may, however, be less familiar. The qualifications of the chaplain are the same as for any Christian minister plus an understanding of the mind-set of the athlete.

Chaplaincy is initially often viewed with suspicion by sportspeople. On hearing of the appointment of a chaplain to his club one professional footballer commented, "I've seen a lot of things in my time but a vicar in the football club. . ."

Chaplains are sometimes greeted and treated as totem poles. Superstition is, of course, very common in sports teams, and the wise chaplain would be well advised to distinguish between his role and any success the club might enjoy; if he does not he might soon prove to be a great disappointment.

At the Olympic Games in Seoul in 1988 the two British chaplains were able to get to know the GB ladies hockey squad reasonably well because the vice-captain, Violet McBride, was a committed Christian. They watched most of the games, but eventually had to miss one for other duties. GB lost the game and one of the girls later commented, "We looked for you in the crowd; where were you?"

At other times the chaplain's presence is better understood and welcomed. At the Commonwealth Games in Auckland in 1990 the Canadian chaplain was a tremendous help to the team. One of the Canadian synchronized swimmers arrived in New Zealand to discover that her father had died. The team management was glad to have somebody who knew about bereavement on hand to help. The girl went on to win the gold medal.

On Saturday 15 April 1989, football's greatest tragedy of the modern era occurred at Hillsborough, in Sheffield. 95 people died in the crush at the start of the FA Cup semi-final between Liverpool and

Nottingham Forest. Gordon Wilson, who had been
chaplain to Sheffield Wednesday for ten years when
the disaster happened, was not at the game.

Just after 3 p.m. Gordon was on his way from a
wedding to the reception. As he turned on the radio
and heard the news of what was happening at
Hillsborough, he sent his wife on to the reception,
telling her that he would join her later. He did not
get home until 3.30 a.m. and was back at the ground
by 8.00 a.m.

Gordon takes up the story:

As I walked into Hillsborough at 3.20, I met the
fire chief. I was asked to help set up a crisis centre.
Out of chaos we tried to set up an information
centre where people could come to get information. Initially when anyone arrived at the centre
we had to distinguish people offering help from
people needing help. We attached a social worker
and a minister to groups who were looking for
someone. Their instructions were to stay with the
group until they found the person. That went on
from shortly after 3 until 11 p.m. In some cases we
took people home. My role was really just being
there and being available.

Reflecting on the incident a year later at a conference
of football club chaplains, he said:

If ever there was an incident which illustrated the

need for football club chaplaincy it was Hillsborough.

BIBLICAL BASIS
What is the Biblical basis of chaplaincy? Chaplaincy comes within the scope of the great commission: "Therefore go and make disciples of all nations" (Matthew 28:19) or "you will be my witnesses in Jersualem, and in all Judea and Samaria and to the ends of the earth (Acts 1:8). The purpose is to reach people for Christ.

The example of Jesus who "made himself nothing, taking the very nature of a servant" (Philippians 2:5) and even washed the disciples' feet (John 13:14–17) are also relevant.

The chaplain's witness comes just by being around to show another life style, by showing care, love and Christian compassion.

There are many types of sports chaplaincy work and even within one type there will be contrasting characteristics. Amidst the variety it is possible, at this stage of development, to identify six "models" of sports chaplaincy. Conscious that they might be out of date as soon as this book is published we will now examine each in turn.

(i) THE SPORTS EVENT MODEL
Most great sports events – "The Games" – operate under the guidance of the Olympic Charter which provides for religious freedom, guaranteeing oppor-

tunity for competitors to maintain their religious observations.

In practice this means that there is a team of chaplains at the Games. Generally speaking other religions will also have their representatives available to the athletes.

With the increase of sports ministry around the world it is becoming possible to staff these village chapels with men and women who have an ongoing ministry to the athletes.

(ii) THE TOUR MODEL

A great deal of professional sport is really professional entertainment. Troops of players tour the world, or a part of the world, playing each other over and over again. Tennis and golf are the best examples of this kind of thing, but we could include badminton, eventing, track and field and probably many other sports as well.

To provide effective pastoral support to players on this kind of tour the chaplain has to be available to travel on the tour for at least some of the time. It is expensive and time-consuming.

(iii) THE NATIONAL TEAM MODEL

In many team sports, especially those played outside the USA, the focus of attention is the Test Match or International where one nation pits its best against another. One only has to think of the highly charged atmosphere of an England v Scotland football match at Wembley or England cricketers lined up against Australia at Lords or the South African rugby team carrying the hopes of their nation against the New Zealand All Blacks at Ellis Park, Johannesburg to understand how these great encounters affect entire nations.

These are very pressured occasions in which a chaplain can and should be the available friend and counsellor they need; someone to whom they can speak in confidence and yet someone with no axe to grind, no money to make, and no interest in publicity.

(iv) THE BRITISH MODEL

In the UK over the last twenty years a model of sports chaplaincy has developed which is characteristically British. A minister of a local church has either taken the initiative to forge links with a local football club or been encouraged to do so. In many cases this has led to the appointment of the minister as the club chaplain. In other situations the "chaplaincy" role exists without the official title of chaplain being used.

As we have seen there is a great need for ongoing pastoral care within the world of sport. In football for instance players, often very young players, are exposed to fame, relative fortune and long leisure hours. The potential for making wrong choices is clear. A guiding hand or a listening ear can be very helpful.

This model of chaplaincy also links sports ministry with the local church. It has long been a clear policy of Christians in Sport in the UK to give maximum support to the local church and stand with it in its mission. The world of professional sport has traditionally been a no-go area for the local church but the chaplaincy programme is bridging the gap.

The club chaplain must make regular, at least weekly, visits to the club, just as he might drop in on a local hospital, school, industry or old people's home. He will quickly get to know the office staff and management who will as trust develops appraise him of people who could do with some help or encouragement.

Occasionally he might travel to an away match with the team and stay in the team hotel – always a great way of getting to know people. As soon as anyone is injured or in hospital he will be there caring, praying and supporting.

The key to successful local club chaplaincy is servanthood. It is peculiarly British because it is slow to develop and unsensational in both its impact and appeal. The opportunities for direct evangelism exist, but it will often be inappropriate to be too aggressive in discussion of spiritual things. What the chaplain can do is to pray for and befriend players and their families, introduce them to Christian fellowship and give them the opportunity to hear the Gospel within the context of the local church from which he comes.

(v) THE AMERICAN MODEL

In the 60s and 70s a programme of "chapel" services

began in American Football. A need was recognized
and an opportunity taken to develop a network of
speakers who conducted a brief Bible teaching and
prayer meeting for a team before games in the NFL.
Initially very few pros attended but it has grown
remarkably and now every team has its "chapel". The
team chaplain's principal task is the organization of
this chapel. He must organize a room, extend invitations and arrange for a speaker. Linking the programme with other sports ministers active in the
States the "chapel" programme has seen large num-
bers of players come to faith in Christ and then grow
in their knowledge of God.

(vi) THE AUSTRALIAN MODEL
"Down under" the Australian sports ministry (Special
Life Oriented Ministries – SLM) has gone even
further. The Director of SLM locates and appoints a
minister as chaplain and then informs the club of that
appointment. He also communicates regularly with
the sports officials in his country, keeping everyone
informed of SLM work; but he reserves the right of
appointment unlike the English model which gives
the club that prerogative.

The advantage of this method is that it can quickly
develop a network of chaplains. The disadvantage is
that without the acceptance and approval of those to
whom they go their access is very limited.

CHAPTER SIX

The Olympic Games

Held every four years, the Olympic Games represent the culmination of sporting achievement. Athletes sacrifice everything in the preceding four-year period for the chance of winning a medal or even just for the honour of taking part. The Olympics, more than any other sporting event, has managed to find a place for the true amateur, the representative of the tiny nation alongside the millionaire superstar American sprinter. The Olympics too have an unrivalled pedigree.

The Olympic Games which began in 776 BC in Greece were the clearest expression of the origin of organized sport. The games gathered competitors together on one site and integrated sport into a wider festival. However, they were taken seriously. In Sparta youths were taken from their families and reared in austere conditions in preparation for combat, the forerunner of the modern training camp!

If we think that the ancient games were pure and wholesome and that we have spoilt them in the modern era, it may come as a surprise to us to learn that the Emperor Theodosius banned the Games in

AD 393 amidst boycotts, bribery and corruption!

The Olympic Games were originally religious in character. Like the Pythian, the Isthmian, the Nemean, and the Athenaic, they were sacred festivals, integral aspects of the religious life of the ancient Hellenes. In the words of one scholar, "The Olympic games were sacred games, staged in a sacred place and at a sacred festival; they were a religious act in honour of the deity. Those who took part did so in order to serve the god and the prizes which they won came from the god. . . The Olympic games had their roots in religion." The games at Olympia were in homage to Zeus. Those of Corinth – the Isthmian games – were sacred to Poseidon, while Apollo was worshipped by the runners and wrestlers of Delphi and Nemea.

The modern Olympic movement was revived in 1896 in Athens mainly under the influence of Baron Pierre de Coubertin, who had the encouragement of Pope Pius X. The first modern Olympics were a huge success. While the athletic standards were modest, the enthusiasm and good sportsmanship of the Greek spectators ensured the success of the event.

In recent years the Olympics have often been marred by world events. The 1968 Olympics in Mexico are remembered as much for the Black Power salutes by the American athletes as for David Hemery's superlative victory in the 400 metres hurdles final or Bob Beamen's world record in the long jump which was to stand for over twenty years.

In 1972 the Munich Olympics were the object of a terrorist attack. A group of Palestinian terrorists broke into the village and killed two Israeli competitors and took a further nine hostage. A gun battle at the airport as the Palestinians tried to make their escape left all nine Israeli hostages, five terrorists and a policeman dead. The Games were suspended for a day and a half and a memorial service held.

The 1976 Games were boycotted by a group of African nations in protest at New Zealand's links with South Africa. Moscow was the venue in 1980. However the Soviet invasion of Afghanistan led to a boycott of the Games by the USA and some other nations. As far as Britain was concerned there was a partial boycott with individuals participating but some team sports being boycotted. With the 1984 Games being in Los Angeles, the USSR staged a counter-boycott.

The 1988 Games in Seoul, Korea, were overshadowed by one event. Ben Johnson won the gold medal in the 100 metres, surprisingly beating the reigning champion Carl Lewis. Then Johnson tested positive, was disqualified, stripped of his medal and sent home in disgrace.

Olympics 1992

Barcelona was an inspired choice for the Games of the 25th Olympiad. A vibrant and colourful city with spectacular architecture and the famous Ramblas promenade running down from the heart of the city to the port, which bustles with boats large and small. Towering over the port is Montjuic, at the top of which stands the Olympic Stadium. The steep climb up Montjuic each evening was made easier by the escalators – a luxury denied the marathon runners – and the slow descent after the day's competition was enlivened by the dancing fountains accompanied by a fantastic music and light show.

Inside the stadium, the atmosphere was tremendous – even though the Spaniards had a habit of whistling and jeering false starts and gave Khalid Skah the rudest of responses after that controversial 10,000 metres. The Games were full of incident and accident – Gail Devers falling over the last barrier when leading the 100 metres hurdles, Carl Lewis' revenge in the long jump, the gold medals of Christie and Gunnell, the downfall of the three hottest favourites, Messrs Morceli, Johnson and Bubka.

Arguably the highlight of the 1992 Games was the men's 400 metres hurdles. For Kriss Akabusi to crown a great career with an Olympic medal and another British record was a tremendous achievement, but the race itself belonged to Kevin Young, who smashed the world record of the great Ed Moses on his way to the gold medal.

Kriss Akabusi's Olympics

Barcelona was Kriss Akabusi's third Olympics. In 1984 in Los Angeles, he was a 400 metres flat runner who did not make the final. However he came away with a silver medal in the 4×400 metres hurdles.

By 1988 Kriss was a hurdler coming sixth in the 400 metres hurdles and also running in the relay team that was unable to match the performance of 1984, coming fifth in the final.

In the years from 1988 to 1992 Akabusi's stock rose. He collected European and Commonwealth Gold Medals, a bronze medal in the World Championship and was ranked third in the world. The British 4×400 metres relay team approached the Olympics as World Champions, having taken gold in Tokyo in 1991. However Kriss was 33 – nearer 34 if the truth be known – could he continue to improve or would age finally catch up with him? Let him take up the story.

Initially when I went to the Olympic Games I was just hoping to get a medal. But as the Games started I got quite excited as I thought maybe I could win this time round. In the heats and the semi-final nobody looked that terrific. But in the end as history will see I came third and now I'm very happy that I came third and got a medal. I had hoped while I was there that maybe I might have got a gold.

On the day of the final, I was pretty excited – this is it – the finals had come. I got back to my marks and I was very confident actually. In the heats I had run particularly well and I felt very good and thought maybe I could win this time.

I went as hard as I could but by the time I got to hurdle five the American, Kevin Young, came flying past me and I thought, "Oh my gosh, I'm having a bad one". At this point it would have been easy to panic – either to try to catch Young and burn myself out or to give up – then as I got round the bend I worked really hard and I realized I wasn't running that bad because it was just Kevin Young who was ahead of me.

I got to the last hurdle late and Winthrop Graham came past me as well, but the last 100 I knew that if I didn't make any mistakes I was going to hold on to my bronze medal. I think by the time I got to hurdle 10 that's all I was thinking about – holding on to my bronze medal rather than to want to catch anybody else.

After the 400 hurdles came the relay. After our gold medal in the World Championships at Tokyo in 1991, a great deal was expected of us at the Olympics. But by the time we came to the relay we had a few tired legs out there and I think to be honest we knew that it was not going to be as easy as last time. It was difficult to win in Tokyo but we knew we had the ability to win because the Americans did not have their best team in Tokyo, they were very complacent, they thought they could put any four out to beat us.

This time round the Americans had four guys who could go under 44 seconds and we didn't have one guy who could do that. We'd lost Derek Redmond who was the British record holder a week earlier. So we knew we were up against it. We were very tired when we got there. I did not think I would be the best man to run this time and tried to get out of it – there were a couple of other young guys who hadn't run during that week. In the end we came third. We felt we should have got silver but that was the measure of how tired we really were.

Jo Edens

Kriss Akabusi competed for Olympic gold in a packed stadium covered live on television around the world. He had spent the previous few years working full-time with the Olympics as the goal. Jo Edens also competed in the Olympics in 1988 and 1992. There the similarity with Akabusi ends.

Jo competed in the Olympic archery. She has no sponsorship to speak off. Competitions are either at weekends or she has to take days off from work. She found it great to be there but stressful as well.

I enjoyed the Olympics. Everything was very well

organized. My performance was OK but the standard was so high that my placing was lower than I had hoped for.

For many people – the athletes for example – the Olympics are just another event. They are used to the big crowds, the publicity, etc. For the archer it is quite different. Your sport is normally very low-profile, truly amateur. When you go to the Olympics everything is different and intimidating. Without meaning to family and friends can put you under pressure by having too high expectations of you.

Derek Redmond

The semi-final of the men's 400 metres produced probably the most poignant moment of the 1992 Games. Derek Redmond, the British record holder was running. Redmond had to pull out of the previous Olympics at the last minute with injury. The next four years had seen him have a succession of operations, mainly for Achilles tendon problems. In the 1991 World Championship he made no impact on the individual race but was in the historic UK 4×400 metres relay team which won the gold.

Now at last it was beginning to happen. In the heat in Barcelona he was flying. He started well in the semi-final then after 150 metres he pulled up sharply, clutching his hamstring. The Olympic dream was over. Minutes later he was weeping inconsolably on trackside. Anyone who was surprised by his tears has no idea of the effort involved in getting to the stage of competing for an Olympic medal or the utter desolation of seeing years of work disintegrate in seconds.

Violet McBride

Violet McBride is a teacher in Kilkeel, Northern Ireland. In her spare time she plays hockey. Violet had one great ambition in hockey, to play in the Olympics. It took her twelve years but she made it. Violet takes up the story.

The 1988 Olympic Games were without question the highlight of my hockey career. To realize what it meant to me you have to understand that I had trained and prepared for twelve years with the aim of making the Olympics. The Great Britain team was due to take part in the 1980 Games in Moscow. Then the USSR invaded Afghanistan and the authorities decided not to compete in the team sports so we didn't go.

We failed to qualify in 1984. As 1988 approached I was 33 and I knew that it was my last chance. It was make or break. In the period leading up to the Olympics I was, as far as school commitments would allow, a full-time hockey player. I was determined to get everything I could out of the experience of going to the Olympics.

We reached the semi-finals losing to Korea and also lost the third place play-off against Holland so we didn't get a medal. To be honest that was not a great disappointment to me. Having waited so long for a chance to get to the Olympics, it was great just to take part. The third-place game proved to be my last international appearance. As the captain, Barbara Hambly, was injured I had the privilage of captaining the Great Britain team in that game, a nice way to finish.

What made the Olympics different from any other hockey tournament that I've played in was the presence of people from other sports. Daley Thompson was always a great hero of mine and it was great to meet him – he even played volleyball with us in the training camp in Japan. I enjoyed watching the track events when I had a chance. I'll never forget seeing Flo-Jo run, I've never seen such a complete athlete.

Violet's impression of the Olympic experience underlines further the pressure for the true amateur to compete in the limelight.

The Olympics were a fantastic experience but to be honest I didn't enjoy it all that much as a hockey competition. There was so much pressure on you all the time, pressure to be in the team, pressure to do well. I was relieved when it was all over and

glad to be back home and playing club hockey and
back in the school where I teach.

Olympic chaplaincy

Freedom of worship is enshrined in the Olympic
charter. As a result a chapel and a team of chaplains
are provided at the Games.

The purpose of chaplaincy at a major sports event
includes:

— providing regular opportunities for worship for
  those who want it;

— providing Bibles and Christian literature on
  demand;

— providing friendship to overseas visitors, fellowship for those who are already believers;

— counselling is available on demand.

The key to successful Olympic chaplaincy is friendship, human concern and pastoral concern.

To appreciate what it is like you need to picture
the scene in the competitors' village, a totally cosmo-
politan, spotlessly clean area where competitors jog
or lounge around in tracksuits waiting for their event.
Each competitor's nationality is easy to determine
from the uniform.

You need also to appreciate the size of the oper-
ation. There will be some 15,000 competitors and

officials from more than 150 countries representing about thirty different sports.

As you follow signs to the "religious" or "Christian" centre, you find a chapel, counselling rooms, a quiet area, a bookstall, facilities for refreshments and generally a welcoming attitude.

A typical day for the chaplains might include a meeting for prayer, praise and a report back from other chaplains, a morning walk through the village making contacts in coffee bars or snooker halls, keeping an appointment with a believer who needs encouragement, accompanying an individual or a group to training, taking an athlete shopping, arranging hospitality with a local Christian family for an athlete, praying with a discouraged chaplain for new openings, eating meals with athletes, leading or attending evening service in the chapel.

Andrew Wingfield Digby, director of Christians in Sport, was chief chaplain at Seoul in 1988. He stressed the service element in the work.

> It is often a case of just being there as a Christian minister, making oneself available to whoever needs help, encouragement, prayer or just company. There are opportunities to share one's faith but in general it is not appropriate, at least by the chaplains. The brief is: be available but don't get in the way.

While evangelism may not be appropriate for the chaplains, there are no such restrictions on the competitors. This distinction was well illustrated in Seoul. The chaplains recall inviting Kriss Akabusi and other British athletes to the chapel services which were planned for each day.

Kriss replied, "Certainly we want to meet every day but let's do it out in the open so that everyone can join us as they want." Such an initiative by the chaplains would have been frowned upon by the Games Committee but as it was the athletes' idea, no problem. The meeting took place every evening at 6 p.m.

A particularly memorable meeting was held on the night before the 4×400 metres relay final, with three of the finalists represented – Kriss Akabusi from UK, Innocent Egbunike of Nigeria and America's Danny Everett.

As each one prayed Egbunike's prayer was "Lord, I don't ask that I should win, but please, please don't let me finish behind Akabusi". The meeting ended in chaotic laughter.

Violet McBride was another who was glad of the presence of the chaplains.

In the midst of all the activity and pressure, I appreciated the chaplains. When I arrived there was a note from one of the chaplains waiting for me, saying that they were around. I went to the chapel services as often as I could. Two teammates – neither of them Christians – often came with me. One of them was injured before the competition.

The chaplains prayed for her and she recovered and was able to play in the last match.

A particular opportunity provided by chaplaincy at a major sports event is seeing athletes from countries which have few Christians being brought into contact with Christianity, perhaps for the first time.

The following examples from the 1991 World Student Games in Sheffield – all of them could as easily have happened at an Olympic Games – illustrate the point. Members of the Iranian team coming to request Bibles in their own language – often coming late at night so that no one would know, a Bulgarian athlete receiving a Bible in Bulgarian for the first time and the Chinese student who came into the chapel enquiring in faltering English, "Want to become Christian, you have application form?"

In Barcelona there was a daily Bible Study for members of the British team. Mark McAllister who travels with the athletes and leads the Bible Studies summarized what happened.

These Olympics marked a milestone for the Christian presence in the British team. It was at the Seoul Olympics just four years ago that it began with just three or four. In the intervening years over twenty athletes have attended our gatherings. Some have come and gone, others have wavered in their commitment, but prayer and Bible study have become an expected element of major competitions.

In Barcelona there were none of the open-air

meetings of Seoul, but most days a group of about half a dozen got together. Together we looked at some of the New Testament characters who met Jesus.

Conclusion

One incident from the 1988 Games in Seoul encapsulates in a nutshell so much of the Olympic spirit. Gerald Williams who was covering the Games for BBC watched the Marathon finish on the television in his hotel room. Then an hour or two later he set out to walk to the stadium for the closing ceremony.

As he neared the stadium he was overtaken by a Marathon runner still plodding on towards the finish, oblivious to the fact that the medal-winners had long gone. The incident so spoke to Gerald of the Olympic spirit, of taking part rather than winning, of perseverance in sport, in life and in the Christian life that it seemed to be included in all his sermons.

CHAPTER SEVEN

Never on Sunday

An issue which the Christian sportsperson has to face
is Sunday competition. Can the Christian, with a clear
conscience, be involved in a sport which requires
participation on Sundays?

Background

The film *Chariots of Fire* brought the Sunday sport
issue to the attention of the Christian public in a new
way. The film featured two athletes from the 1920s,
Harold Abrahams and Eric Liddell. The Sunday
Sports Bill which was presented to the House of
Lords in 1987 and the subsequent Sunday Trading
Bills have kept the issue on the public agenda.

The Sunday Sports Bill sought to "permit the
admission of persons by the payment of money or
tickets sold for money to tracks (defined as races,
athletic sports or other sporting events) on Sundays.

The bill was defeated and the status quo maintained. While promoters of sports events are not per-
mitted to charge admission money on Sundays, the

same end is achieved by selling tickets in advance, making the purchase of a programme a condition of entrance, etc. Sunday sport continues largely unhindered by the legislative framework currently in place.

The first Sunday racing took place at Doncaster in 1992. An added dimension of the Sunday racing issue is the question of off-course betting. Many people would find Sunday opening of High Street betting shops undesirable.

Biblical material

What is the Biblical material on the subject? The first reference to the Sabbath is in Genesis 2: "On the seventh day God rested . . . and God blessed the seventh day and made it holy." In the wilderness the people were told to gather twice as much manna as normal on the sixth day because "tomorrow is to be a day of rest, a holy Sabbath to the Lord" (Exodus 16:21ff). The principle is enshrined in the ten commandments: "Remember the Sabbath day by keeping it holy" (Exodus 20:8). Moreover the Sabbath is a sign of the covenant between God and Israel (Exodus 31:12–18).

In the New Testament the Pharisees challenged Jesus and His disciples about picking ears of corn on the Sabbath. Jesus' response is: "The Sabbath was made for man, not man for the Sabbath so the Son of Man is Lord even of the Sabbath" (Mark 2:27–3:6).

Paul writes to the Colossians, "Do not let anyone judge you by what you eat or drink or with regard to a religious festival, a new moon celebration or a sabbath day. These are a shadow of things that were to come. The reality, however, is found in Christ" (Colossians 2:16, 17). And again in Romans 14:5 Paul writes, "One man considers one day more sacred than another, another man considers every day alike. Each one should be fully convinced in his own mind."

Keep Sunday Special

The case for a Sunday free of sport is put by such bodies as the "Keep Sunday Special" campaign and the "Lord's Day Observance Society". In a 1989 publication by the Lord's Day Observance Society, *The Lord's Day, 100 leaders speak out* the foreword states:

Throughout the history of this nation, we have been privileged to possess a great Christian and national heritage. . . One of the most important aspects of our great heritage is the Lord's Day. In this publication we have listed one hundred statements from leading people, including church leaders, politicians, doctors and sportsmen, who have testified to the importance of the Lord's Day.

It is our prayer that as you read their testimonies, they may stimulate you to make an even firmer stand for the promotion and preservation of this

God-given gift which has been a blessing to our people in the past and which will be, we trust, for generations to come.

The case for keeping Sunday special, as set out in *Why Keep Sunday Special*, published by the Jubilee Centre in 1985, depends more on the Sabbath principle than on an argument developed from proof texts. It is stated:

A day of rest is part of God's plan for all men. It is part of what is best for man. Setting Sunday apart helps ensure that we make time in the week to rest. . . A day in the week when almost everybody is free from work is an important way to help family life and friendships to flourish, by giving people time to spend together.

Interestingly the case does not rest on what is often seen as the basis for the Christian attitude to Sunday. The authors state that the reason for keeping Sunday special is

NOT because Sunday is the New Testament Sabbath. In our view it is not . . . [and NOT because] it is a sin to work on Sunday. Working on Sunday is not necessarily sinful. Paul tells us that whether we keep Sunday special or not is a matter of individual conscience. Working on Sunday is only wrong if it leads us to neglect the underlying principles of love for God and love for our neighbour.

The authors of *Why Keep Sunday Special* conclude this section of their argument by noting that while Jesus and the apostles kept a day special in the week, there is no command to God's people to do likewise.

Eric Liddell

The historical champion of abstinence from Sunday sport is Eric Liddell, who is featured in the film *Chariots of Fire*. According to the film Liddell was on his way to the 1924 Olympic Games in Paris when he discovered that the final of the 100 metres race was to be held on a Sunday. He decided that he would not run and even a meeting wih the Prince of Wales on the cross-Channel ferry would not convince him to change his mind.

The facts are a little different. Liddell knew months in advance what the Olympic schedule would be and accordingly made his decision to run the 200 and 400 rather than the 100 and 200 metres. He gained a bronze in the 200 and the gold in the 400. The win was made the more potent by a note handed to him before the race: "He who honours me I will honour" 1 Samuel 2:30.

In her book *The Flying Scotsman*, Sally Magnusson wrote:

"I'm not running", he said and nothing would

budge him. He didn't make a fuss but was absolutely firm about it.

The Sabbath was God's day and he would not run. Not even in the Olympic Games. . . Reverence for the Sabbath was as natural to Eric as breathing and infinitely more precious than a gold medal.

In *The Lord's Day, 100 leaders speak out*, there is a longer quote from Eric Liddell:

There are many people today who think of those who honour Sunday in an old-fashioned way as killjoys. They feel that during the years of their youth they ought to have a chance to "have their fling". Give me the day of rest, when all the savours of organized games can be put on one side and all life's joys will be greater because of it. To me personally it is a time of communion and fellowship with God, a time of quiet, in fact a time of recreation by fellowship with God. I believe that Sunday as we have had it in the past is one of the greatest helps in a young man's life to keep all that is noblest, truest and best.

David Sheppard, now Anglican bishop of Liverpool, was in the 60s a test cricketer. In his book *Parson's Pitch*, he stated his position on Sunday sport:

When my faith in Christ became a real thing, I started to think differently about Sunday cricket. Until then I had frequently played in Sunday club matches or charity games. Now I wanted my faith to grow. I needed time to worship God . . . time to think, time to relax and talk to other Christians.

Accordingly David Sheppard decided not to play cricket on Sundays any more.

Similarly many other sporting heroes of the past have taken their stand. In the 1930s Jack Hobbs, arguably the greatest batsman in history, refused to play in a Sunday match on a tour to India. The match was rearranged. Dorothy Round, the 1934 Wimbledon Ladies Singles Champion said, "I shall never consent to play any tennis on Sundays".

Traditional Christian attitudes

Many Christians today believe that this is the correct attitude. Last year a reader wrote to the *Christian Herald*:

I was pleased to see the letter on the subject of Sunday sport recently. It seems very regrettable that so many sporting events are now arranged to take place on the Lord's Day. I feel concerned about Christians being tempted to watch such events. Many years ago Eric Liddell set a good example when he refused to run in the Olympics on a Sunday and other sportsmen and women have taken a similar stand. With such good examples before us, surely Christians today should seek to stand firm on this issue.

Another reader wrote saying:

What a pity we do not hear more of those Christians who refuse to play their sport on a Sunday. We need Christians in Sport to make a stand for the Lord and his day.

However, is it a realistic attitude? Can the attitudes of the 1920s and 1930s be applied in the 1990s? Today Sunday sport is much more prevalent that it was. Dorothy Round could win Wimbledon in the 1930s, holding to her principles of never on Sunday. Similarly Jack Hobbs and David Sheppard could opt out of Sunday cricket. Is that a realistic option in 1993?

The sporting calendar

It is impossible to generalize about the extent of Sunday play in sport. There is great variety from sport to sport. In tennis, for example, most tournaments – including Wimbledon – involve Sunday play. There would be no contract in professional cricket for the player who was unavailable on Sundays. Over 90 per cent of professional golf tournaments involve Sunday play. In rugby union there are hardly any Sunday fixtures. However, even where there are no Sunday matches, most amateur sports hold their training sessions over the weekend, including Sunday. As a result it is necessary to look at a few individual sports to see how the Sunday issue applies in that sport.

Football

At a time when there is a choice of Sunday football on TV most weeks, it may be hard for us to believe what a recent phenomenon Sunday football is. It effectively started on 15 February 1981 – although there had been some Sunday games in 1974 during the three-day week. Now Sunday games are common-place, often but not always to suit TV schedules. Football cannot be shown live on a Saturday afternoon as the televised game could affect the attendance at live games. Therefore a different slot has to be found for it. Friday night and Monday night have been tried but Sunday afternoon has become the preferred time.

One of the first Christian players who had to face the issue of Sunday play was Alan West who was at that time Luton Town captain. Luton were to play Leyton Orient on a Sunday. The press got hold of the story and amazingly most of the national papers ran the story of how Alan would have to miss church to play for Luton. In the end Alan was not selected for the match – perhaps the manager felt that his heart was not really in the game, who knows.

Alan did subsequently play on the occasional Sunday, reluctantly but without going against his

conscience. What saddened him was the critical attitude of Christians. He said:

> I decided to play after giving it a lot of thought
> and prayer, realizing that it was my job, not just
> something I was doing for fun, and that I was under
> contract.
>
> I felt that if doctors and nurses, police or bus-
> drivers could do their jobs on a Sunday, what was
> the difference between them and me? It is funny,
> though, when members of my church who work at
> Vauxhall do Sunday shifts, no-one says a word. Yet
> when I do my job on a Sunday everyone is up in
> arms.

Shortly after the first Sunday game, Alan was due to
speak in a another church. He received a curt letter
cancelling the invitation. "We do not want anyone
who plays Sunday football speaking in our church",
the letter said.

Cricket

Mark Frost is a professional cricketer. He is by no
means a world class player although he did once drive
West Indian fast bowler, Courtenay Walsh for a
straight 4! He is an honest professional who had two
seasons at Surrey and now plays for Glamorgan. Inevitably he plays Sunday cricket when required. The
Sunday league is well supported and as such brings

in welcome revenue to the counties.

Mark is a committed Christian who is sure that cricket is part of God's plan for his life. He sees himself as a witness in the world of professional cricket. Experience has taught him that being there in the dressing room as a Christian is often enough to provoke questions about Christianity without Mark having to look for angles.

If he wants to keep his job Mark has no choice about Sunday cricket.

There are no professional cricketers who can say to the captain: "Sorry, I can't play Sundays, I go to church." Most captains would reply: "OK then play in the second team all year." The choice for me is play or no job. Despite what some people may think, I have thought deeply about the issue.

At one stage I started getting hostile mail, often anonymous, questioning my commitment to Christ and condemning me for desecrating the Lord's Day. My response is that if I were not in the dressing room, there would be no Christian presence and no conversations about spiritual things. Moreover looking at the Bible, one reads in Matthew 12 how Jesus healed on the Sabbath and when the Pharisees criticized him, he stated that a) it is lawful to do good and b) He is Lord of the Sabbath. I take reassurance from Colossians 2 where Paul writes: "Do not let anyone judge you by what you eat or drink or with regard to a New

Moon celebration or a Sabbath day" and when criticism comes, Paul goes on, "Do not let anyone who delights in false humility . . . disqualify you for the prize."

As Mark says, the most frustrating thing is when those who criticize you assume that you haven't thought about the issues.

Hockey

Violet McBride played hockey for years without ever being confronted with the Sunday issue. Then when she was in the running for selection for the Great Britain squad for the 1988 Olympics she found that many of the training sessions were on Sundays, so much so that she began to consider whether or not she should continue to be involved.

> Missing church regularly on Sundays was a problem for me. I asked myself was I doing the right thing. I prayed about whether or not I should continue to seek selection for the Olympic team. In the next few weeks I had more opportunities to talk to teammates about God than ever before. I felt very much that God was saying, "I want you to be involved in the team."

During the Games Violet was encouraged that the other players were very much aware that she was a

Christian and accepted her for it. When she attended the chapel services, two other players – neither of them Christians – often came with her. At other times someone would see her Bible and daily reading guide and ask: "Well, what's the message for today?" At other times players told her, "You will have to pray for us".

Throughout the Olympic period Violet had constant encouragements:

> While I never seek to button-hole anyone, in small ways I often had opportunities to share my Christian principles and values. As Mark Frost asked, would any of this have happened had Violet decided to opt out of the GB hockey squad on the Sunday issue?

Track and field

Two British athletes who have declined to compete on Sundays are Barrington Williams and Jonathan Edwards. The two came to prominence in 1988, when each was prepared to sacrifice an Olympic place rather than compromise. The media took every opportunity to brand them as the latter-day Eric Liddells.

Their circumstances were slightly different. Barrington Williams was at that time our leading long jumper and also a sprinter. However, the long jump was without doubt his main event. When the Olympic timetable was published, the long jump was set for a Sunday. Barrington decided to seek Olympic selection only in the 100 metres. Against the odds, he came third in the Olympic trials and made the team.

For Jonathan, the issue was not the Olympic event itself but the British Olympic trials which had scheduled the Triple Jump for a Sunday. The system was that the first two in the trials gained automatic selection for the Olympics with the third place to be filled at the discretion of the selectors.

In human terms there was no doubt that Jonathan's best chance of selection lay in competing in the trials. He chose not to. The story had a happy ending when Jonathan gained the discretionary place and was off to the Olympics.

In 1991 Jonathan established himself as the UK number one triple jumper and also managed to beat his own personal best for the event. However it was also a year of frustration for him. The two major events of the year were the World Championships and the Europa Cup. In both, the Triple Jump was scheduled for a Sunday. Jonathan came under a certain amount of pressure, was told that he was letting his country down. However, he did not compete.

In an interview shown on ITN's *News at Ten* programme shortly before the 1991 World Championships, Jonathan explained his position.

As a Christian, God comes first in my life and keeping Sunday special is not so much following a rigid rule. It is just a way of showing that God is first in my life and not my athletics.

In 1992 Jonathan had a growing conviction that God was calling him to change his stance and jump on Sundays. Knowing that some people would be surprised at the decision Jonathan took the trouble to write down his reasons, sharing honestly the soul-searching that it involved. The article which appeared in the *Christians in Sport* magazine and was quoted elsewhere, included the following:

When I learnt that every major competition of '93 was to be on a Sunday I was stunned. More than ever I knew that God was calling me to serve Him as an athlete through being a part of the Christian presence within the British Athletics team and being a witness to my fellow athletes and yet here was the door slammed in my face.

That evening I felt God telling me to visit a friend to talk to him about the situation and he reminded me of a dream that another friend had dreamt, concerning me. In this dream I was at the end of the runway waiting to jump but I was frustrated because there were lots of people in my way; but when the people were moved I ran down the runway and made a great leap.

Since the Olympics I had felt a release within myself to jump on Sunday but didn't know it was the right thing. I felt that God was saying to me, through this dream, that it was fear of man that was stopping me making the decision. The great leap, I felt, wasn't an actual jump, as my season was long over, but rather a leap of faith. Up until now not jumping on Sunday was an act of witness, now I was to be a witness by competing on Sunday. I believe that the leap of faith God was calling me to make was to jump on Sunday. Humanly I can see many persuasive and good arguments to remain not jumping on Sunday, yet God exhorts us to walk by faith and not by sight.

To say that I have no fear of this step would be untrue. To bring dishonour to my God would break my heart, and yet I know that if God has called me, then this step will bring glory to His name. The same friend who I visited shared with me that God had recently said to him: "It is better to be stoned walking in God's ways than to live in the chains of fear and compromise." Much of my wisdom tells me: don't to it. Yet God's word says: "Trust in the Lord with all your heart and lean not on your own understanding. In all your ways acknowledge Him and He will make your paths straight."

My initial decision not to jump on a Sunday was a big one. I love my athletics but knew that God was calling me to make a stand for Him to show what my priorities were. The issue was never is it right or wrong to jump on a Sunday *per se*, rather was it right for me. I decided not to compete on Sundays as a way of saying that my faith in God was more important than athletics.

This decision to compete on Sundays is a big one but it is essentially no different from the original decision not to jump on Sundays. God, I believe, is again calling me to make a stand for Him. Now I believe God is calling me to serve Him by competing on Sunday. This time the path before me does not seem as clear yet I know that He who called me is faithful and He will bring it to pass.

Rugby

Michael Jones the New Zealand rugby player has for the past few years been, in most people's opinion, the best wing forward in the world. Michael is another sportsperson who does not play on Sunday. In the 1987 World Cup, Michael was good enough to play in the quarter-final, opt out of the Sunday semi-final and still be chosen for the final.

The schedule for the 1991 World Cup in Europe was less accommodating. The way the tournament unfolded – call it the luck of the draw or the hand of God – left New Zealand playing more Sunday games than any other team. In fact three out of their six matches, including the quarter-final and semi-final were on Sundays.

In the end Michael Jones played in only one match in the World Cup which really mattered, their opening game when New Zealand defeated England, effectively sealing their place in the quarter-final. Jones scored the decisive try. Beyond that he played only in a one-sided match against the USA and the match to decide third place, after New Zealand had been knocked out of the main competition.

Opinions differed on Michael's decision to make himself unavailable for the Sunday games. Some saw it as the supreme example of a Christian sportsman putting his principles first and saying that his faith in God – and his view of Sunday – were more important than a game of rugby, even a World Cup semi-final. Others saw it as a waste of his talent, arguably denying his team the chance of winning the World Cup.

He came under pressure to play on Sundays. Some people even suggested to him that Sunday in England is Monday in New Zealand – because of the time difference. Michael answered that in a Radio Wales interview.

> You can't trick God. You can't muck around with Him. It is where you are at the time and Sunday wherever you are, which is the day that has been put aside for church and fellowship.

Michael also shared his aim in taking his stand:

> When you stop playing rugby people easily forget you and one thing I would like to be remembered

for is as a person who put God first, before rugby. If it's been worthwhile doing that then it is worthwhile and I feel that it's important that people who never would have heard about God have done so through my stand because it's brought attention to it. If I've been able to show people that there is obviously a God who must exist or else someone wouldn't be prepared to do that, then I feel it's been worth it. If I can do that I'm happy.

Golf

Almost all professional golf tournaments involve Sunday play. This is another sport where a player must choose between playing on Sunday and finding another job.

Kitrina Douglas, a player on the Women's Professional Golf Tour, feels that she has taken on board the Sabbath principle but is still free to play in tournaments which involve Sunday play.

> I don't really have a problem because I have taken it to the Lord and He has given me a clear conscience. The concept is one day to be holy to the Lord. If I play golf on Sunday then I try to find other times in the week to rest, put God first and spend time with Him.

Kitrina also finds the players' weekly Bible Study a

help. As she puts it, "The players can't get to church, so we bring church to them."

Bernhard Langer's question "how can we grow as Christians if we never get to church on a Sunday?", referred to earlier is still relevant. Part of the answer is through fellowship at other times.

Incidentally Bernhard's involvement in the tour, with its Sunday play, has led to the establishment of a regular Bible Study as a witness to other players. Moreover on occasions there have been opportunities to hold public services on the course on the Sunday morning before play commenced.

Sunday sport at club level

The issue does not just affect top-level performers. Parents of talented teenagers often find their children reach a stage in the sport where no progress to the next stage can be made without being available for coaching or competition on Sunday.

Take the case of a talented sixteen-year-old runner. He believes that his ability is God-given and wants to develop it to the full and to glorify God through it. The local athletics club, however, have one of their main training sessions on a Sunday morning.

He shares the problem with the leaders of his church who tell him that he "shouldn't put pleasure before worship" and that the church would not allow him to remain in fellowship if he committed himself to the athletics club.

What is he to do? Are the church leaders right to use their authority to insist that he "seeks first the kingdom of God" or are they adding their own traditions to the Scriptures? Can it not equally be argued that by seeking to use his God-given talent to the full he is glorifying God and into the bargain having opportunities to witness for God in what may be a very pagan sports club?

As Shirl Hoffman suggests:

when the ark of the covenant was brought into Jerusalem, Scriptures say that David "danced before the Lord with all his might" 2 Samuel 6:14. On the surface at least, there seemed no good reason why the same jubilation couldn't have been expressed by throwing the javelin or running the 1500 metres.[1]

Conclusion

In trying to sum up the issues relating to Sunday sport which face the Christian, it has to be recognized that it is an issue on which Christians differ.

Moreover it is at times difficult to identify exactly what the issue is. For some it seems Sunday sport is wrong in absolute terms. It is sinful to play sport on Sunday. However, it has to be said that such an argument is difficult to sustain from the Bible. The preservation of the traditional British Sunday may be a desirable objective. However it is hardly a fundamental point of the faith.

If, however, the argument concerns priorities, the putting of "worship before pleasure", then participation in a sporting event only becomes an issue when it clashes with church attendance. There is no problem with participation in a sporting event which takes place before or after church attendance. It may even be acceptable for the meeting together with other Christians to take place at another time of the week.

If we believe that the Scriptures teach that every day is special, every day is holy to the Lord, every day is to be used for Him and every activity is part of our witness to the saving power of Jesus Christ, we may feel that there is no issue over Sunday sport.

We have noted too that there are Christian sportspeople who do not necessarily think that Sunday play is wrong, but have chosen not to participate in Sunday sport as a way of saying that their relationship with God is more important than their sport.

In our summing-up it may also be helpful to distinguish three categories – the professional, the top amateur and the "for fun only" player, while recognizing that the distinctions between the three are not always entirely clear cut.

For the professional the bottom line is: Do I honour my contract and do my job on Sunday or do I choose a different job where there is no necessity of Sunday work? This dilemma, however, is not unique to sport but applies equally to doctors, nurses, train drivers, postmen, police shift workers and all who may be required to work on Sundays. Incidentally I am aware of no professional sportsperson who has decided never to take part in Sunday sport.

For amateurs for whom sport is a "hobby", albeit a hobby which is pursued with great sacrifice and dedication, there is scope for choice. While one's sporting career may be hindered by the decision to opt out of Sunday competition, as amateurs they are free to make this choice. Their livelihood does not depend on it. They can choose to use the Sunday issue to make a public statement about the importance of their Christian faith in relation to the importance of their sport.

For club-level competitors who find that particular opportunities to practise their sport come only on Sunday, the issue is different. It is essentially one of priorities.

There are no easy answers to the issue of Sunday sport. It is an area where each Christian in sport must decide according to conscience before God. It is an issue on which individuals will reach different decisions.

The Church should accommodate the position of the Lord's Day Observance Society, but should equally be able to understand and support Christians who take part in competitive sport on Sunday.

CHAPTER EIGHT

Does God Care Who Wins?

Introduction

Is there a higher proportion of people in the world of sport with a religious faith than in the rest of society or does it just seem that way? The "born-again phenomenon" has certainly been well investigated.

Ray Stubbs introduced a feature on the subject of sport and religion for the BBC *On the Line* programme in 1991 with the following words:

> When the new Archbishop of Canterbury was enthroned, it heralded a new era of evangelism for the Church. In the 90s it's cool to be Christian. In the vanguard of this charismatic army are the footballers, cricketers, tennis players, golfers and athletes who have all united behind the born-again banner. A case of Onward Christian Sportsmen.

The programme featured a number of Christian sportspeople, including Cyrille Regis, Kriss Akabusi and Bernhard Langer, looking at how they related faith to their sport.

Perhaps even more so in the USA, the "disproportionately high number of athletes in big-time sport with a Christian faith has become a matter of curiosity to social commentators". Two examples of this are a recent book, *Sport and Religion*, a collection of essays edited by Shirl Hoffman – on which we will draw heavily in this chapter – and a series of articles by Dana Scarton in the Pittsburgh Press under the title "The New Testament – Christianity's March on Sports".

Sport as a religion

The similarities between "sport" and "religion" have been noted by many people. Both have the power to galvanize a community and to incite people to fanaticism. Both have sacred times and places – be it Saturday afternoon or Sunday morning, church or the sports stadium. Participants dress in a particular way – be it football scarves or Sunday best.

When the Hillsborough disaster occurred, which cost the lives of 95 fans, Liverpool's Anfield Stadium became a shrine where fans came to pay their respects to the deceased and to leave floral and other tributes.

Several American commentators see sport as the new religion of America. The resources being pumped into it, the amount of TV coverage, its importance to the advertising industry all give sport a central position in modern American society.

James Baker calls American Football "America's

newest indigenous religion . . . it has all the trappings of a cult: coloured banners, armies of good and evil, fanatical fans, cosmic sphere, even its own miniskirted vestal virgins [cheerleaders] to fan the flames." Spectators are not left out of Baker's model. Their role "is not unlike a Latin High Mass performed by professionals for the edification and instruction of those deemed by the Heavenly Commissioner unworthy to participate personally".[1]

For others doing sport is a form of religion. Hal Higdon quotes a Jewish convert to running, who says, "Now I know what it feels like to be a born-again Baptist. I try to convert my non-running friends."[2]

Higdon writes further of the "phenomenon of the born-again runner" for whom running is the most important part of life, dominating the weekend as church activities will dominate Sunday for the Christian family. For some runners there is in addition an intense mystical experience in the running, drawing near to God while running, all the more so when running in areas of natural beauty.

It has too been suggested that the injunction to the Christian to "present your bodies as a living sacrifice, holy and pleasing to God" is relevant to runners and that a body "capable of carrying its owner through the 26 miles 385 yards of a marathon might be considered more pleasing to God than a body which through the owner's indolence has been allowed to deteriorate into a blob of flesh that quivers from the strain of moving from couch to kitchen for another beer".

While there are certainly superficial parallels between sport and religion, it is inadequate to equate the two. There are aspects of sport which have a religious aspect or provoke a religious fervour. The differences are well summed up in another quote from Hoffman:

> Religion is serious and solemn, and concerns things eternal; it acknowledges human weakness and dependence, it inspires contrition and adoration. By comparison, sport is frivolous, amusing and concerns things ephemeral, manifesting itself in acts of confidence, domination, and not infrequently intimidation.[3]

Other commentators have taken it even further wondering how religious people reconcile their beliefs with the violence in sport and even suggesting that it is as inappropriate to pray before a football game as to have "the priest say a few words just before the lions come out to eat the good Christians".

Playing sport can be a religious experience in some sense. If we believe that our bodies and our abilities are a gift from God, then playing sport can be an act of worship just as much as any other activity. Peter Brock of the New England Patriots talks of playing football in that spirit.

I now approach Sunday afternoons as a worship

service. The Bible tells me "present your body as
a living and holy sacrifice, acceptable to God, which
is your spiritual service or worship". God has
blessed me with a large body and great strength
and the ability to play this difficult game. My
responsibility is to play to 100 per cent of my ability
as a way of thanking him for what he has done for
me.

Superstition

Sportspeople are notoriously superstitious. If you win
there is the belief that the win was derived in some
way from the routine leading up to the game. The
routine must therefore be repeated next week.

This situation is described by ice hockey player,
Dennis Abgrall (quoted by Mari Womack in *Why
athletes need ritual*).

When you win, you try not to change anything.
Nothing. You do everything exactly as you did the
whole day of your win. Beginning from the time
you get up, was your window/door left open? Get
up on the same side of the bed. Eat the same
meals, at the same places – home or at the same
restaurant – nothing extra. If your salad was dry,
order it dry again; if you had a large milk, then
again; if your steak was ordered medium, then
again; no dessert, and so on. You leave at the same

time, take the same routes, park in the same place, enter through the same door, and prepare for the finale – game time – with the accent on precision.

When Sunderland won the FA Cup in 1973, manager Bob Stokoe's lucky suit – worn for every round of the Cup – got its share of the credit.

Other superstition rituals include the order in which a player puts on his kit (e.g. left sock before the right) or the order in which players run onto the field (i.e. always last, second last etc.). In baseball it is taboo to say "no hitter" in case the mere mention causes it to happen. Players will wear a particular medallion as a good luck charm. We have heard of ice hockey players, banned from wearing medallions around their neck for reasons of safety, taping them inside their shoes!

Golfers are no less superstitious. Jack Nicklaus usually played with three pennies in his pocket; Al Geiberger used a penny as a ball-marker, always ensuring that the president's eyes faced the hole and so on.

The most unusual superstition recorded perhaps involves the throwing of a dead octopus onto the ice at an ice-hockey game! In 1952 a local fish merchant and ice hockey buff started the tradition when the Detroit Red Wings needed eight victories to be champions – the idea being that the eight tentacles would bring eight victories. When the Red Wings achieved their eight victories, the superstition was established.

Every time he went into bat Alan Knott used to touch the bails before facing his first ball – as a kind of concentration trigger. One match, the opposition wicket-keeper stood with his hands protecting the wicket to prevent Knott from touching them. Realizing that people thought it was a superstition Alan never did it again.

All of this seems harmless enough even if it is curious to find such primitive rituals given such credence in our sophisticated society. What may be more disturbing is the use of religion as a form of superstition. There is some evidence of players using religious practices as a good luck charm.

Hoffman recounts an incident during the 1978 football season, when the Houston Oilers visited the Pittsburgh Steelers, they recruited a local minister to deliver the pre-game talk and prayer. When the Oilers pulled off an unexpected victory, the upshot was that when the two teams played each other again both teams asked the minister to do the pre-match prayers. "The minister opted to pray for the Steelers, who then won, extending his streak to 2–0!"[4]

British football chaplains sometimes get drawn into this. The chaplain who visits the players on the Friday before a good result will be expected the following Friday. Equally a chaplain who has seen the team lose successive games may be asked not to come to any more games.

The chapel system

Most professional sports teams in America have a chaplain. A principal function of the chaplain is to organize a match-day chapel service for the players.

The origins of chapel are traced back to the early 70s when the advent of Sunday games made it difficult for players to attend church services. In 1973 a New York based umbrella organization, Baseball Chapel Incorporated, was founded. It now provides about 200 speakers nationwise for team chapels. Twenty years on in addition to the top league it is estimated that 80 per cent of players in the minor league attend chapel. The situation in American Football and Basketball is not dissimilar.

From a Christian perspective, it is encouraging to think of a great number of top players taking time out before the big game to focus their thoughts on God and to give thanks to him. Moreover there are documented cases of players coming to faith in Christ and then growing in their knowledge of God through the chapel programme.

However, our study would also seem to indicate that chapel services have been caught up in the whole phenomenon of the interface between sport and religion.

Lori Rotenberk in an article called "Pray ball", published in *Sport and Religion* gives this account of a chapel service:

Above, the organ plays "Take me out to the ball game. . ." while below, in the clubhouses of the great American stadiums, the chaplains stand.

The shower drains and weight machines are their pulpits, half-clad ballplayers the flock. Surrounded by the clink of cleats, the bonk of the Louisville Sluggers and the strings of profanity, they wind up for their pitch. The delivery is pure heaven as it curves and drops low for a strike landing smack in their mitts.

"I can do all things through Christ who strengthens me." That's Philippians – not Phillies – 4:13.

And from Chicago to Cincinnati, from Pittsburgh to St Pete, baseball players bow their heads in worship, God's message belting forth from the storage rooms, trainer's rooms and locker rooms cum chapels:

"No, men, the diamond is not sacred ground. Remember, the world doesn't revolve around this here little ball. There is only one Perfect Player, one True Game Plan. So, hit the dust, break up the double play. Get the team a run, but give the Glory to God!"

And thus ends Baseball Chapel, a 20-minute pre-game exercise of faith performed in ballparks nationwide each Sunday by an estimated 4,000 major and minor league players, coaches, trainers and managers.[5]

The impression given here of the chapel is less of an act of worship to an omnipotent God than of a ritual part of the psychological build-up to the game, similar perhaps to the *haka* war dance performed by the New Zealand rugby team just before their matches. Moreover a survey of American players and coaches in the 60s indicated that more than half believed that pre-match prayers would affect the result.

The following comments of Bill Glass, a former football player turned minister, on his approach to speaking at a chapel service rather confirms this view. "When I speak to a team before a game I find I am talking a Christian line but I am also talking motivation, I know that most players aren't into a heavy spiritual content so you don't preach a sermon like you would in church. I talk about how I used to get myself ready for a game. It's the Christian power of positive thinking."

Further evidence of this is found in the fact that one American coach, George Allen, insisted that his players attended chapel because he found that it did more "to produce togetherness and mutual respect than anything else I've found in 21 years of coaching". Some commentators have noted too the inconsistency in the coach who insists that players attend pre-match chapel but who would never consider going to church himself.

For many, of course, the chapel is quite sincere, not occasions for asking for a victory as much as asking God's presence and blessing on the event. Those who

have integrated their faith into all aspects of their lives
and who customarily pray before important events in
their lives are also likely to pray before a big game
as anything else.

How do we make sense of this dichotomy? Perhaps
we must acknowledge that chapel is different things
to different people. There is no doubt that for some it
is part of the superstitious, ritual process of psyching
oneself up for the match. However that does not
detract from the sincerity of other players in wishing
to come aside and focus on their creator for a short
period, even on match day. In any case who is to say
that the motivation of the average Sunday morning
church congregation is any more pure?

Yelping about God

Boxer Marvin Frazier was knocked out by Larry
Holmes in a televised fight. When he had recovered
he was asked by NBC sportscaster Dick Enberg about
how the knockout occurred. Frazier replied: "First I
give praise to my Lord and Savior Jesus Christ for
giving me the opportunity to be a witness for him. . ."
Only then did he answer the question!

After winning the Baseball World Series, Gary
Carter went before the cameras to say: "My only
dream was to give glory and praise to Jesus Christ."[6]

This practice – what Hoffman calles "The ubiqui-
tous unsolicited post-game theological endorsement"

is becoming commonplace in press conferences after sports events in America. It has also been called "yelping about God".

The player may ask if it is legitimate to use the occasion to promote Niké, Gatorade, Goodyear or whoever your sponsor happens to be – both by having it in large letters across your kit and by expressing public thanks to the sponsor – why may the Christian athlete not also acknowledge his maker?

When a group of New York Giants and Buffalo Bills players knelt in a circle and prayed at the end of Superbowl XXV, it evoked similar mixed reactions.

The motivation may be pure. The Christian athlete longs to share what is most precious to him/her. The sporting success provides the platform. Questions to be asked include: does it trivialize the faith to have it shouted in a "First of all I want to thank Jesus Christ. . ." formula and does it communicate something to the listeners or just turn them off?

This issue was discussed in the Pittsburgh Press articles. Betsy King is one of America's top golfers. She is also a Christian. She feels that there is antagonism towards her Christian faith among the media. "I mean I've actually seen reporters get up and walk out of the press tent when I start talking about my faith."

Angus McEachran, editor of the *Pittsburgh Press*, gave the journalists' view. He insists that there is no separate policy for dealing with Christianity. "The first question we would always ask is how germane it is to the story." The journalist's goal is to write a factual, readable story. If the person's religious beliefs seem pertinent they are included. If not, they are omitted.

To that Betsy King adds: "My viewpoint is that if they're just going to write about golf and they do it with everyone, that's fine. But if they write about someone's [belief in] reincarnation then they have to write about my faith."

Incidentally Betsy King's point about reincarnation is probably a reference to an American golfer who, on her first visit to the UK to play in the British Women's Open, announced that the country was very familiar to her as she was in fact the reincarnation of King Arthur! This was widely reported in the British press. King won the tournament but there was no mention of her Christian faith.

The important point being made here is that if you have orthodox Christian beliefs no-one is interested but if you announce that you have won the tournament because you worship your dog or because you are in fact King Arthur, then it is news.

The answer is perhaps moderation. There have been many occasions when Christian sportspeople have been able to speak to the press about their faith in an honest and sensitive fashion, making the point when it is relevant. Going into the press conference determined to make a statement about one's faith in answer to the first question – whatever its subject – seems unnecessary.

God made me win

A more extreme version of "yelping about God" is the player who attributes the winning touchdown to divine intervention. An outstanding example of this was Floyd Patterson, on his defeat of Archie Moore to win the world heavyweight championship: "I just hit him again and the Lord did the rest."

When the baseball home run is attributed to God it does of course beg the question of how God decides whether he is for the hitter or the pitcher that particular day.

On this issue the author unashamedly sides with Jay Wilson, chaplain to the Pittsburgh Pirates and Steelers who expresses it beautifully in the Pittsburg Press: "Spiritually God doesn't give a rip if I win or lose, He's more concerned with my character than with anything else."

The Gospel according to sport

One aspect of the sport and religion interface is the emergence of a Christian sports subculture, which uses sporting analogy to present the Gospel in a format of object lessons. One example is from a book by Larry Jones, *Practice to win: Conditioning that works in sports and in all of your life*. The following excerpt is fairly typical of the approach of the book:

In basketball, the player who commits a foul causes his team to be penalized. And after his fifth personal foul, he is not allowed to play any more. . .

The same is true in the game of life. Those who try to take shortcuts, to bend the rules, never get away with it for long. Sooner or later they foul out – of school, in marriage, in business and in their Christian walk.

When you make a violation on the basketball court, the referee blows the whistle. When you make a violation in your walk with Christ, the Holy Spirit calls "foul".

James Baker refers to "the handsome guys who go round telling church camps how it feels to win with Jesus". He summarizes their "incipient form of a football theology" as follows:

> God is a great general manger. Jesus is a terrific coach. Life is a terrifically great game if you're playing for Those Two. It's OK to gamble on fourth and one [a reference to going for a touchdown on the fourth down and risking losing possession], but don't gamble with your soul. And that's about it.[7]

Wes Neal, working on the premise that Biblical principles were the ideal foundation for athletic training, prepared a manual on "How do I lift weights the way God wants me to lift them?" Turning to the Bible he found that there were specific answers to such

questions. He compiled in a training manual, a list of
Bible verses that seemed to apply directly to various
dilemmas in the life of an athlete, including anger,
depression, money and team spirit. Under the section
for Contract Negotiations he referred the athlete to
Luke 3:14:

> . . . and soldiers likewise demanded of him, saying
> What shall we do? and he said to them, Do violence
> to no man, neither accuse any falsely and be con-
> tent with your wages.

While for most people this approach is simplistic
beyond belief, doing justice neither to the "full coun-
sel of God, nor to the world of sport", aspects of it
emerge in incipient form in some much more respect-
able circles. One example of this is the view that the
parallels between the requirements of sport and of
Christianity make one a good preparation for the
other.

This view is expressed by Tom Landry, for many
years head coach of the Dallas Cowboys:

> I think this is where football and Christianity have
> a very close relationship, because to live a Christian
> life a person has to be just as disciplined in the
> things he does as a player does to be successful in
> football. We feel we can build character and
> develop good traits in athletes and this is why I
> think an athlete is such a great candidate for Jesus
> Christ.

Being a winner for God

Does having a religious or Christian faith make you a better player? There is certainly a strong case for being wholehearted. As Paul wrote in Colossians: "Whatever you do, work at it with all your heart, as working for the Lord" (Colossians 3:23)

However, there is a school of thought found in some American circles which sees Christianity as the supreme motivation for success on the sportsfield. The following quotations illustrate the point:

> There is also this attitude among Christian athletes, even though I'm a Christian I can play a rough brand of football. In effect as a Christian I ought to play an even rougher brand than anyone else. I represent the greatest cause on earth and I should represent this cause with excellence in sports. Obviously I would play fair and square, but tough.
>
> Bill Glass, *Expect to Win*

> If I could put Jesus Christ into my shoes he would be the most aggressive and intense performer on the field. He would win every time.
>
> Top baseball pitcher Dave Dravechy

Whether this is the Jesus of the New Testament or an embodiment of the American dream is very much open to question. The all-American Jesus portrayed here is perhaps rather at odds with the biblical Jesus of Nazareth whose kingdom was not of this world. There is surely a danger in this whole area of seeing Christianity as just one more gimmick to help win the vital game.

Equally worrying is the attempt by some athletes to see the supreme effort of the competitor as a parallel to Christ's sufferings at Calvary, reminding himself that "Christ was no quitter". Wes Neal quotes a wrestler motivating himself by reminding himself "I had to do the same thing Jesus did when He went out to finish the task His Father had called Him to do".

Using sport to advance the Kingdom of God

An aspect of what we might call American evangelical triumphalism is "winning for God", the idea that success on the sportsfield can also help God's cause. A fine example of this is the attitude of Oral Roberts towards sport at the university which takes his name:

> Just playing the game is not enough. It's all right to lose some, but I'm not much for losing. We're geared up for winning here.

The author has to agree with Shirl Hoffman's slightly cynical view of this attitude.

> Presumably the Lord likes to see his favorite team

win and trouncing the heathens from state college up the road proves in its own inexplicable way that the Institution's position on theology was right all along.[8]

Sports ministry is in its infancy. We should therefore not be surprised to find that mainstream thinking is occasionally accompanied by the downright wacky! We are well advised to take the apostle John's advice and test everything.

Conclusion

The message of this book is that sport is part of God's creation and as such is to be enjoyed by his creation. We can do no better than to repeat the words of Eric Liddell from the introduction: "God made me for a purpose but he also made me fast and when I run I feel his pleasure."

Sport is an area about which people become passionate. It is most definitely more than a game. At times the result of one match takes on an importance out of all proportion to its real significance. With so much at stake it is hardly surprising that the "win at all costs" mentality has been allowed not only to raise its ugly head but to be nurtured and encouraged by players and coaches alike. Sportsmen and women are just ordinary people. They are not the superheroes and demigods that we like to make them. They are no better and no worse than anyone else. With the provisos only that they experience many of the successes and pressure of life at a younger age than do the captains of industry for example. Moreover top sportspeople live their lives in the goldfish-bowl environment which means that the slightest slip is a public slip.

The relationship between sport and Christianity is a complex one. Some of the claims about how Jesus would have reacted in a particular baseball situation may make us cringe. Those who appear to go to a sports event to evangelize, for example spending the day kneeling by the golf tee with their John 3:16 banner in the hope of catching the TV camera, rather than to enjoy the event for its own sake seem equally to be abusing God's gift of sport.

The hope and prayer of the Christians in Sport movement is to see more and more top sportspeople living consistent godly lives in the cauldron of professional sport, seeking to take seriously the teaching of Jesus and to work out its implications in the situations that they meet. In this way they will give glory to God and be a witness to their peers, without needing always to be "yelping about God".

Similarly we long to see at grass-roots level, every church having a sports programme, seeing how sport can be used to fulfil the great commission of making disciples of all nations. Christian players in their clubs can make an impact by the way they conduct themselves.

If this book can help even a little in the fulfilment of these goals, it will have been worth while.

APPENDIX 1

SPORTS MINISTRY

What is sports ministry?

What is "sports ministry"? It is a concept which is easier to exemplify than to define. It is wide-ranging and all-embracing. It is the interaction between the Christian Church and the world of sport at all levels.

Sports ministry is . . . a Bible Study at an athletics meeting, it is forming a church football team, it is chaplaincy to the Olympic Games, it is a church keep-fit class, it is a Sunday service on the 18th green during an international golf tournament, it is a fun-run raising money for a Third World project, it is being a witness in your team and much more beside.

A vast number of different activities have been tried in the UK alone over the years. The following 25 examples illustrate the diversity of initiatives which can be accommodated under the umbrella of sports ministry.

Examples

1 **Outreach dinners** – held in sports clubs, restaurants, hotels, church halls and private homes, to which sportspeople are invited to hear the good news about Jesus.

2 **Sports services** – in which a local church puts on a special service with a sporting flavour and invites the local sporting community to hear the Gospel.

3 **Sports demonstrations** – such as table tennis, golf, squash organized in local youth or sports clubs.

4 **Golf Days and Clinics** – to which Christian golfers invite their friends to play a round of golf, watch an instructional clinic and hear an after-dinner speaker.

5 **Christian teams** – have been entered in both secular and church leagues. While this is probably most common in football, there are an increasing number of examples from other sports.

6 **Matches** – particularly in cricket, have been taking place against local villages, schools and colleges.

7 **Chaplains** – have been appointed to football, cricket and rugby clubs as well as to the men's and women's professional golf tours, the British athletics scene and the England cricket team.

8 **Keep fit/aerobics classes** – have been run by

churches as a service to the community and an outreach opportunity.

9 **Sports Evenings** – where a church hires a local sports centre involving people in sporting activities such as five-a-side football, badminton, indoor cricket, squash, swimming etc., sometimes with a talk afterwards.

10 **Exhibitions** – a Christian stand in the trade exhibition has been mounted at sports events, e.g. the All England Badminton Championship, Snooker World Cup, Speedway, Equestrian 3-day events, etc.

11 **School visits** – there are many examples of both one-off and ongoing ministry in schools or even a school mission, in which events are centred around sport.

12 **Local Media** – have been supplied with articles and interviews with Christian sportspeople and events. Sports sections have been contributed to local newspapers and Christian news-sheets.

13 **Prisons** – Christian sports teams have played against inmates and spoken in chapel services.

14 **Men's breakfasts** – have been addressed by a Christian sportsperson.

15 **Bike for Bibles** – events have been used to raise money for the Bible Society.

16 **Pastoral support** – has been offered to leading sportspeople in friendship, telephone calls and fellowship.

17 **Hospitality** – has been provided for high-profile sportspeople especially from overseas when competing in this country e.g. Wimbledon, Eastbourne, Birmingham Tennis Tournaments, Women's Professional Golf Tour.

18 **Hospital visits** – have been arranged to injured players.

19 **Fun-runs** – have been arranged to raise funds for worthy causes.

20 **Prayer** – special prayer has been held for the world of sport, locally and world-wide.

21 **International tours** – have been held including two cricket tours to India, a rugby tour to Spain, a hockey tour to Jersey, football tours to India, Bangladesh and all over Europe. Aims of such tours include encouraging the players in their own faith, presenting Christ to the opposition and raising money for local charitable projects.

22 **Literature** – the production of Christian literature aimed at sportspeople, written in sporting language and often incorporating the testimony of a Christian sportsperson.

23 **Testimony** – top-level sportspeople using the plat-

form that their achievements in sport give them to talk about their faith in outreach events or through the secular media.

24 **Major-event chaplaincy** – at the Rugby World Cup, the World Student Games, Olympics, Commonwealth Games, etc.

25 **Evangelistic Supper Parties** – where the Christian invites team-mates to supper to discuss the claims of Christ.

Origins

The origins of sports ministry in Britain can be traced back to the early 1970s when a number of Christian men and women with a love for and involvement in sport began to meet regularly together.

The essential message which that group grasped and became excited about was:

a. that sport was something that could be done, and used, "Christianly". It was not separate from their Christian lives, but integral to them. As they began to live by this new realization they saw sportspeople becoming Christians.

b. That sport was a vehicle by which the great commission of Jesus could be furthered. Sport is a global "language" and sportspeople can cross cultural, linguistic, social, racial and economic barriers in a unique way. Areas of the world that are "closed" to traditional missionaries are "open" to sportspeople.

Christians in Sport

Sports ministry was defined in British form in 1980 when Christians in Sport was established as an independent registered charity. The formal objectives as stated in the Trust Deed are:

The object of the Charity is the advancement of the Christian Religion among people in sport and in furtherance of the above object the Trustees shall have the following powers:

a. To proclaim the Christian message of salvation to sportspeople and others involved in various aspects of sport.

b. To provide Christian teaching for and to strengthen the faith of Christians already involved in sport.

c. To help and encourage Christians in sport to share their faith with other people in sport and in society generally.

d. To help and encourage Christians in sport to show their faith by relieving poverty, advancing education and providing recreational facilities for those in need.

Why sports ministry?

Each year there is a Christians in Sport service at the Kensington Temple, an international charismatic church in West London. During the service one year the church drama team did a sketch which included the memorable line "Christians in Sport this week. I suppose next week it will be Christians in heavy metal-work".

The serious point behind the drama is: what is the justification for a distinctive Christian ministry to sport? The question could even be put: What has sport got to do with the Church in its spiritual ministry and function? In fact the Church has traditionally viewed sport with suspicion.

Rodger Oswald, until recently pastor of Los Gatos Christian Church in California, in an unpublished paper entitled, "Sports ministry and the church – a philosophy of ministry" gives two answers to these questions:

— Sport is a mission field;

— Sport is a tool to work harvest fields.

In relation to the first point he notes the Church's concern for "unreached fields" in Africa, South America and the far corners of the earth but wonders why the Church does not seem to have a similar concern for "unreached fields" who gather in the sports stadia of America each weekend.

Arguing for sport as a tool for proclaiming the Gospel, he sees sport as a meeting place for millions. He goes on:

> If you want to penetrate a crowd, what better way than for one of the crowd to do it; if you want to reach athletes, what better way than with an athlete? In fact, what did it take for God to reach us? It took the incarnation of Christ.

He concludes by asking if Paul would become a Jew to reach Jews and a Greek to reach Greeks, would he not become an athlete to reach that group?

Categories of ministry

There are several different aspects of sports ministry which have developed in Britain. These include pastoral care, evangelism, local church and student ministry. It may be helpful to look at them separately.

Pastoral care

An important aspect of sports ministry is providing pastoral care for professional sportsmen and women at the highest level in order to help them to be more effective disciples of Christ. That might be meeting them one-to-one because they're new Christians or they've moved clubs and they're in different parts of the country and they need somebody who is available to travel and spend time with them in a way that the local church can't.

The priority, having got to meet them in those situations and helped them and pastored them, is to identify a strong, spiritually alive, local church in which the player can get involved and play a part and where the Bible is taught faithfully.

The role of the sports minister in this context would be to play an interim role often pastorally in these areas. In the longer term it would be a supplementary role to the local church in understanding the nature of sport particularly in a pastoral context and being alongside the local church and helping in that way.

The goal in doing that is that we might help these men and women to identify the mission field which is theirs and theirs alone in professional sport where they are the most effective witnesses for Christ. So we want to offer the help that we can to make them more effective witnesses for Jesus, in a mission field that no-one else can reach as effectively as they can.

Evangelism

MISSIONS
Sport-orientated missions for local churches, schools and local Christians in Sport groups are held regularly all over the country. What sports ministry can offer here which is different to other significant and

valuable mission organizations, is sport. That brings the great advantage of being able to break the barriers very quickly with boys and girls, young people in schools, because not only can one lead assemblies and work in classroom situations talking about being a Christian and answering questions, but also go in and teach football, cricket, hockey and netball and work within the games and PE contexts.

By speaking a universal language of sport the right has been earned much more quickly than without that language to be able to relate easily and to share the Gospel of Jesus in a relevant way in the social context.

DINNERS

Outreach dinners are held at sports clubs or hotels to which sportspeople are invited. The Gospel is then presented in an after-dinner speech format. Jesus went to dinners with sinners and pharisees in order to get to know them. The principle is to take the message to them in an environment where they are comfortable.

PERSONAL APPROACH

The most effective form of evangelism among sportspeople, and everyone else, is personal evangelism when someone tells their friends about their faith in Christ.

Local church

Local churches are increasingly seeing sport as a means of building bridges to the community with a view to reaching the people contacted for Christ. See appendix 2 for full details of local church sports ministry.

Student work

Students, like professional sportspeople, often have high kudos in their social context in university or college if they are successful sportspeople. The Christian student in the university football, rugby, hockey or netball team has an opportunity to be a witness in that team. They have opportunities to win people for Christ – students which other Christian organizations might not get near.

The student Christian group – be it the Christian Union or even a student Christians in Sport group – can help those people in exactly the same way as professionals are supported.

Conclusion

As the working week shortens and leisure time increases, sport will play a more and more important part in our lives. Sport is therefore an increasingly strategic mission field. It is also a significant channel through which the world can be evangelized. As sportsmen and women live godly Christ-centred lives an effective and lasting witness for Christ will be established which will make a great impact on the nation.

APPENDIX 2

Sport and the local church

The Church has always had a rather ambivalent attitude to sport. While several league football clubs have their origins in churches, the view has tended to grow up in the churches throughout the twentieth century that sport is "worldly" and not something that devoted Christians should really be involved in. Furthermore the fact that sport is sometimes played on Sundays lends credence to the view that sport should be viewed with suspicion. The incident discussed in the chapter on Sunday sport where a teenager was told to put "worship before pleasure" shows that this attitude is still prevalent.

On the other hand in recent years sport is increasingly being seen as a way of building bridges to the community, of reaching young people and of bringing unchurched adults within the orbit of the Christian community.

The motivation

The motivation in any local church sports programme
has to be outreach. As Christians we are ambassadors
for Christ. We have been entrusted with the message
of reconciliation and are called to fulfil the great commission to "go and make disciples of all nations"
(Matthew 28:19). Sport and recreation is one way
in which churches can involve and envangelize the
community around them.

Too often evangelism only happens in "set-up" situations – the guest service, big crusades, street preach-
ing, etc. By using sport we can create situations in
which we can talk to people about Jesus as naturally
as about last night's TV programmes.

The Christian sports celebrity

The one way in which many churches would like to
have an involvement in sport is in the form of a visit
from a Christian sports celebrity. The Christians in
Sport office is inundated with requests for Kriss
Akabusi or Cyrille Regis to come and speak.

By and large Christians in Sport resists this pressure, pointing out that being the fastest runner in
Europe, or a first division club's leading goal scorer
does not necessarily make you an accomplished
speaker. Experience has shown that while a celebrity

speaker may attract a bigger than average congregation, this will include a significant number of starseekers from other churches. What is more, the aftermath of the service is much more about getting the star's autograph than finding out about the message.

That said, a number of churches have found that a sports service can be a useful event in the church's programme.

The sports service

Sportspeople's services have been held in various locations. The organizers invite members of local sports clubs. On occasions attempts are made to make the church look as little like a church as possible! Local sports clubs have been invited to have a display or to highlight their sport in the church.

The service is geared to the congregation, for example using well known hymns, avoiding long prayers. The Bible reading can be by a representative of one of the local teams. Where possible a prominent local Christian sportsperson speaks about his/her faith in Christ. The preacher seeks to apply his presentation of the Gospel to an audience that understands sport.

The church sports programme

Increasingly since the Second World War churches have been incorporating sports activities into their programme. However, these have often had no purpose beyond the social enjoyment of the participants. Churches have run badminton clubs of a rather exclusive nature to which outsiders would not have been welcomed.

Similarly churches have played football or cricket against other churches, and in some cases church football leagues have been formed. The Surbiton and District Churches League was founded in the mid–1960s. In addition the National Christian Youth Organizations – Crusaders, Covenanters, Campaigners, etc. have often used sports competitions as part of their programme.

However, in the last few years the idea of using sport as a means of evangelism, of reaching the outsider, serving the community, etc. has begun to develop more explicitly.

Local church sports ministry is effectively a form of "lifestyle evangelism". It differs from other forms of evangelism only in the means which is used to bring people within the orbit of the Christian community. Sport is the common ground between the non-church person and the church.

Sport and recreation provide an opportunity for living out a Christian character. The experience of playing sport with committed Christians should, hopefully, lead the non-church member to ask questions about attitudes, motivation, etc. as well as affording opportunities to the Christians to talk naturally about their faith.

However, as Leonard Browne points out in his booklet, *Sport and Recreation and Evangelism in the Local Church*, "this approach can backfire if Christians fail to act any differently (or actually act worse than) their non-Christian opposition or team-mates".

While it will take most churches in the UK a long time to reach the level of the Peninsula Covenant Church, Redwood City, California, which has a gymnasium, eight floodlit tennis courts, a swimming pool, a basketball court, sauna, steamroom and jacuzzi, run on a commercial basis, there is no reason why any church cannot begin to mount a programme aimed at meeting the needs of the community with a view to winning people for Christ, tailored to their own resources and the needs of their own community.

Even in the American churches which have invested huge sums of money in building and staffing a church sports centre, the struggle to get members to use the facilities for outreach and not just for fun remains.

Leonard Browne suggests the following ten-point plan for getting started in sports ministry.

1. Pray with the church leadership about the possibilities.

2. Appoint someone in the church to lead the work.

3. Assess your church's facilities and resources and see what is possible.

4. Begin in a realistic way, being prepared to build it up slowly.

5. A good way to start is by hiring the local sports centre for a family fun day for church members and friends.

6. Organize occasional events such as a fun-run.

7. Start regular activities such as a keep-fit or aerobics class for mums, with a crèche provided.

8. Form teams in appropriate sports, be it football, hockey, netball or bowls.

9. Use clinics, teaching the skills of particular sports.

10. Seek to use 1–9 above to draw people in with a view to having evangelistic events to which to invite them.

What are the models of local church sport which have worked?

The church football team

Football is one of the commonest sports played at

church level. The number of churches with a football team playing regularly in the UK is certainly in the hundreds. In some cases the team exists solely for the enjoyment of the players as their relaxation. However, increasingly churches are seeing the football team as a way of extending God's Kingdom without in any way lessening the enjoyment.

There are several different approaches to the church football team. One question to be faced at an early stage is who to include in the team. Is it to be exclusively Christian or church based, or is the aim to make friends with outsiders?

Including outsiders in a Christian team is not without its problems. A Christian team for which the author played once included a friend of a friend of a friend in a match. In the first half he punched an opponent, swore at team-mates, argued with the referee. We asked him to leave the field before the ref did. So much for the witness of the Christian team!

Alan Slough, who played nearly six hundred football league games, now runs Torbay Christians in Sport team. Alan sees the team's aim as "to promote good sportsmanship on the pitch and to bring people closer to the Lord". Success on the pitch is important but not enough.

Gary Piper, vicar of St Matthew's, Fulham, says of his church team: "We formed the team to keep in touch with contacts. The aim of the team is evangelism – but we also want to win the league!"

Another issue is whether you play in a Christian or

secular league. Teams of Christians playing against
teams of other Christians in a churches league seems
in danger of missing an opportunity. While a churches
league is probably a good stepping stone, it ultimately
seems desirable for every Christian team to enter a
secular league and aim to be a witness there.

The witness of the Christian team in the secular
league can happen in different ways. Behaviour on
the park is the obvious starting point. The Christian
team must seek to uphold the highest levels of sportsmanship, play fairly, avoid dissent. Some teams make
a point of praying together before the kick-off. A few
teams have prepared a piece of Christian literature
which is given to each player in the opposition. The
leaflet might set out the philosophy of the team and
also include a feature on a prominent Christian footballer and a short presentation of the Gospel.

In thinking about Christian teams, the idea of the
individual Christian playing in a secular team should
not be overlooked. Andy Kelman, a member of Christ
Church, Cockfosters, played football for several years
for East Barnet Old Grammarians in the Southern
Amateur League, and was for part of that time first
team captain, always seeking to relate his faith to his
football. "I see playing football as an important part
of my Christian life. It is my main form of outreach.
I look for opportunities to invite team-mates to things
at church. One year, for example, I brought almost
the entire team to a Christians in Sport outreach
dinner. Now that everyone knows that I am a Christ-

ian, team-mates have begun to ask me questions about my faith."

Keep fit

In our modern society we have become more fitness conscious than ever before. This is an area in which a number of churches have found a way of providing a useful service to the community and making contact with outsiders. The vast majority of keep-fitters are ordinary people seeking to achieve a standard of fitness sufficient for promoting and maintaining general good health, rather than specialists.

The benefits of running keep fit classes are numerous but they must be properly organized in a suitable venue with lots of space, exercise mats and if necessary a crèche and refreshments. An essential is having someone fully qualified to run it. (Details of appropriate qualifications can be obtained from the Sports Council, the RSA or the Keep Fit Association.)

The church needs to be involved (or perhaps a group within the church) if keep fit is to be used as an outreach. While people may come to the church simply for the keep fit, spiritual and emotional problems may emerge. It is therefore helpful to have church members around to listen to their problems, offer advice and generally get alongside them.

A typical programme for a keep-fit class might include:

1. Warm up – gentle stretching.

2. More energetic movements.

3. Aerobic exercises.

4. Cool down.

5. Floor work.

6. Relaxation.

7. Coffee and chat.

8. Depart.

The sessions can also provide a forum for passing on information about forthcoming events in the church. Exercise is a great leveller and helps people to relax with one another and perhaps become more open to find out what these strange churchgoers actually believe.

In an ideal situation showers would be available afterwards. However this is probably not realistic for most churches. Reasonable facilities for washing would, however, be a real asset.

Coaching

Providing coaching in a sport can be a useful way of attracting people. A number of churches have, for example, organized golf lessons in the church hall during the winter months. All you need is a few mats, a net and some plastic practice golf balls and the church hall has been turned into an improvised driving range.

Beyond that all you need is a Christian golf professional to give the tuition.

Golf day

The objective of the golf day is to expose non-Christian men and women to Christian fellowship and the Gospel. A group of Christians representing either a local church or a Christians in Sport regional group invite their non-Christian friends to play a round of golf and attend a dinner in the clubhouse, at which the Gospel is explained in an after-dinner speech format.

Special events

Special events at which a top performer appears can have a considerable impact. One year on the day after the end of golf's Open Championship, Larry Nelson, former US Open champion, made himself available for a golf clinic at Northwood Golf Club. For an hour Larry talked about golf, hit shots and answered questions, and then in the last five minutes was able to share something of his Christian faith.

A similar activity involved a visit by British Open

squash champion Lisa Opie to a squash club where she played the local club champion and afterwards shared her faith at a dinner.

In these events the Christian sportsperson is able to establish their credibility in the clinic and then take the opportunity of sharing their faith. However the number of sportspeople available for this kind of event is very limited.

Youth work

Children's and youth work is another obvious area where coaching can be effectively allied to evangelism. With less and less sports coaching being offered in schools, and clubs often emphasizing winning more than skills acquisition or personal development, there is a need to be met. The church that provides a caring concern for the child along with decent coaching will be appreciated. The potential to develop a link to the local community is also enormous.

Biggin Hill Christian Fellowship

Biggin Hill Christian Fellowship has grown out of a small Baptist chapel into a membership of about three hundred.

Sport plays a major part in the life of many church-members. Sport is not played just as a means of evangelism. It is something which the church members enjoy doing and which, like any other part of their life, is given over to God. They do not allow their sport to be spoiled by the pressure of feeling they should be talking about their faith all the time but as they participate they are open to and expect to have opportunities to talk about what is the most important thing in their lives.

The church runs a golfing society which has a monthly golf day to which church members invite their friends, frequently outsiders, who simply enjoy a good day of golf together with dinner in the evening. While there is no directly "Christian content" the whole day is one of witness in the way in which Christians play and conduct themselves and live.

Not all sporting activities are church organized. Church members with particular interests are encouraged to join local clubs. After all, that is where the people are. They are encouraged to take an active part in the clubs and to get to know as many people as possible. At the last count the church had members of the local golf club, squash club, diving club, etc.

When the new church centre was built a few years ago, it was designed not just to provide a place for Sunday worship, but also facilities for weekday activities. These include a playgroup, youth group, mother and toddlers group, ladies aerobics, men's circuit training, dance, art workshop, dressmaking, Duke of Edinburgh's scheme and many other activities. These are all properly established and run by church members, some of whom have been sponsored by the church to obtain the relevant qualifications.

Cheam

Another church with a developing sports programme is Cheam Baptist in Surrey. For several years now they have run a fairly successful cricket team which includes an annual visit to Bournemouth for one week, staying in the church hall of West Cliff Baptist Church, Westbourne. The church has been most generous and welcoming and the warmth of their Christian love has been felt by all visitors.

During the course of the week they take part in the Sunday services and the open air coffee morning which has given tremendous opportunities to "gossip the Gospel". They have daily Bible study and discussion with prayer in the morning followed by cricket matches in the afternoon or evening.

Whilst the majority of people on the tour are Christians, it is by no means limited to such. Indeed there has been real blessing and encouragement in that some have been helped to faith in the Lord Jesus through the tour.

They also field a football team and a mixed hockey team from time to time. Whilst the standard is not high, nevertheless the enthusiasm runs high and people are ready to play whenever called upon to do so. The highlight for the mixed hockey team has been a trip to Dublin where they have played against Grosvenor Road Baptist Church under floodlights.

During the past twelve months they have introduced bowls and skittles particularly for men, although with the intention of including the ladies later on these occasions.

Recently the church also commenced "Sport on 3" whereby they take over a sports centre on the third Saturday in each month thus playing bowls, table tennis, volleyball, badminton, etc.

On New Year's Eve morning there is a ladies' football match followed by a men's football match, the participants all coming from the congregation and contacts.

As one of the leaders, Peter Heard, puts it, "Whilst there would appear to be no spiritual content in the sports activities, we feel that in playing matches as "unto the Lord" the manner in which the games are played speaks volumes to non-Christians and there is also the opportunity for evangelism."

Conclusion

Many local churches have found that running a sports activity is a useful way of building bridges to the community, of offering a service to the community. It is an opportunity for church members to invite their friends to an activity in the local church which will bring them into contact with Christians and show them that Christians are really just ordinary people. Without being directly preached at they will learn something of the love of Christ.

Experience has shown that the biggest problem can be getting started in a way which attracts people. One-off events at a local swimming pool or sports centre can be good ice-breakers. As things develop it will be a constant challenge to keep the evangelistic objective constantly in focus.

NOTES

Chapter 1

1 "Sport, religion and human well-being" in *Philosophy, Theology and History of Sport and of Physical Activity*, 1978, pp. 143–152.

Chapter 4

1 *Sport and Religion*, p. 276.

Chapter 7

1 *Sport and Religion*, p. 158.

Chapter 8

1 "Are you blocking for me, Jesus". *The Christian Century*, 5 November 1975.
2 Chigdon, Runners' World, 1978.
3 *Sport and Religion*, p. 132.
4 Ibid. p. 137.
5 Pray Ball, *Chicago Sun-Times*, 22 August 1988.
6 *Sport and Religion*, p. 155.
7 "Are you blocking for me, Jesus". *The Christian Century*, 5 November 1975.
8 *Sport and Religion*, p. 154.

INDEX

Index

Index

Index